Christm

Dear Gwendolen,

May you have many, many hours enjoying baking and eating your own homemade cookies!

Love,
Mom & Dad

P.S. Many of the cookie recipes can be changed to gluten free!

cookies

200 inspirational cookie recipes

First published in 2009
Love Food® is an imprint of Parragon Books Ltd

Parragon
Queen Street House
4 Queen Street
Bath BA1 1HE, UK

Copyright © Parragon Books Ltd 2009

Love Food® and the accompanying heart device is a trademark
of Parragon Books Ltd

ISBN: 978-1-4075-6424-1
Printed in China

Created and produced by Ivy Contract

Additional photography: Sian Irvine
Food styling by Jack Sargeson, Anna Irvine, and Maud Eden
New recipes by Susanna Tee with Sarah Banbery and Jacqueline
Bellefontaine

Notes for the Reader
This book uses imperial, metric, and US cup measurements. Follow the
same units of measurement throughout; do not mix imperial and metric.
All spoon measurements are level: teaspoons are assumed to be 5 ml, and
tablespoons are assumed to be 15 ml. Unless otherwise stated, milk is
assumed to be whole, eggs and individual vegetables, such as potatoes, are
medium, and pepper is freshly ground black pepper.

The times given are an approximate guide only. Preparation times differ
according to the techniques used by different people and the cooking
times may also vary from those given as a result of the type of oven used.
Optional ingredients, variations, or serving suggestions have not been
included in the calculations.

Recipes using raw or very lightly cooked eggs should be avoided
by infants, the elderly, pregnant women, convalescents, and anyone with
a chronic condition. Pregnant and breastfeeding women are advised
to avoid eating peanuts and peanut products. People with nut allergies
should be aware that some of the ready-made ingredients used in the
recipes in this book may contain nuts. Always check the packaging
before use.

cookies

200 inspirational cookie recipes

CONSULTANT EDITOR: **Susanna Tee**

Contents

Introduction

The cookies included in this book are easy and enjoyable to make, fun to eat, and great to share whatever the time of day. Every home should have a well-stocked jar of them waiting to be dipped into, and they are the perfect choice for a mid-morning coffee or afternoon tea, at a children's party or on a festive occasion. Whatever the reason, you are sure to find what you are looking for among the 200 delicious goodies that have been gathered together in this collection.

The making of cookies started as a mixture of flour and water that were baked, on both sides, on a griddle in ancient Egypt and the result was a flat, hard cake. To this basic mixture, leaveners were added to make it rise, and then sugar to sweeten it. Wood burning or coal fired domestic ovens were developed and from their humble beginning, cookies and other treats such as pastries, cupcakes, muffins, bars and brownies, which fall somewhere between a cookie and a cake, have evolved.

The star ingredients

Sugar, fat, eggs, flour, and a liquid are the basic ingredients that the majority of the recipes share.

Sugar

Superfine sugar is usually recommended because it dissolves more easily than granulated sugar. Nevertheless, granulated sugar can be used if necessary.

Fat

Butter is the fat that is suggested in most of the recipes, because it adds richness and produces the best flavor. However, margarine can be used as an alternative, and is less expensive. It is important, though, to use a margarine containing not less that 60 percent fat; choose a hard margarine that is described on the package as suitable for baking. The exception is when a recipe calls for a soft margarine. In this instance, all the ingredients are beaten together with an electric mixer until mixed.

Eggs

The size of eggs used in the recipes is medium unless otherwise stated. If possible, use eggs that are at room temperature because cold eggs can cause the mixture to curdle and will result in a less soft mixture.

Flour

The flour used in the recipes may be all-purpose or self-rising. Should you need self-rising flour but only have all-purpose, sift 2½ teaspoons of baking powder into every 1⅔ cups all-purpose flour.

Liquid

The liquid in the recipes is used to bind the ingredients together and is usually milk, eggs, butter, oil, water, or fruit juice.

Assuring success

Almost all the recipes in the book are easy to make. Follow these useful suggestions and you will be guaranteed success every time:

• Preheat the oven for 10–15 minutes before baking, even if the oven manufacturer's instructions suggest that this is not necessary. If you have a fan-assisted oven, reduce the temperature according to their instructions.

• It is important that ingredients are measured accurately, so it is worth investing in good-quality measuring cups and standard measuring spoons.

• Get into the habit of preparing baking sheets and pans before commencing preparation, because mixtures that contain self-rising flour start to activate once the liquid has been added to them and should therefore be baked as soon as possible after they have been prepared.

• When butter or hard margarine needs to be softened before blending with another ingredient, either remove it from the refrigerator and let stand at room temperature for about 1 hour, or cut into cubes, place in a bowl, and microwave on High for 10 seconds, until softened slightly. Be careful not to let it melt.

• It is not necessary to sift flour to facilitate even mixing unless you are combining several dry ingredients.

• Where dough has to be refrigerated to make it firmer and easier to handle, you can speed this up by wrapping the dough in parchment paper and placing in the freezer for a third of the time that you would normally refrigerate it.

• Do not overbeat cookie batters because this can make them rise too much and sink when they cool.

• Always place cookie dough on cold baking sheets to prevent the dough from spreading excessively and browning too much around the edges. When making a large quantity of cookies, let the baking sheet cool for a few minutes in between batches.

• Bake cookies on nonstick baking sheets or line them with parchment paper but, unless specified in the recipe, do not grease the sheets because the cookies will spread excessively, become too thin, and brown too quickly around the edges.

• Place cookies well apart on the baking sheet to allow room for them to spread during cooking. Unless they are particularly large, a gap of 2 inches/5 cm is usually enough.

• Position baking sheets on the middle rack of the oven for even browning.

• Unless otherwise stated, transfer cookies to a wire rack as soon as they are firm enough to handle and let cool. This will let the steam evaporate and prevent them from becoming soggy.

Equipment & helpful techniques

To make any of the recipes in this book requires very little special equipment and, in many cases, improvisation can be helpful! Nevertheless, here are some suggestions that you may find useful:

● Use your hands! Dampen them slightly when shaping cookies into a ball.

● A hand-held electric mixer is useful for whisking and beating mixtures together but, failing this, use a balloon whisk for whisking and a wooden spoon for creaming.

● When making bar cookies, recipes that specify a particular size of pan can equally be made in a pan with different dimensions but with the same capacity.

● Use a food processor for rubbing fat into flour, but when the eggs or liquid are added, make sure you blend them quickly, because overworked dough will be tough.

● When preparing a pan for baking bar cookies, especially one that is not shallow, line with parchment paper, letting it hang over the edge of the pan. This makes it easier when lifting and removing the cookies later.

● If a recipe asks for toasted nuts and you do not have any, you can toast them yourself. Preheat the oven to 350°F/180°C. Spread the nuts in a single layer on a baking sheet and cook in the preheated oven for 5–10 minutes, turning and watching them carefully until golden brown.

To melt chocolate

Many of the recipes require you to melt chocolate in a heatproof bowl set over a saucepan of simmering water. This is the safest way to melt it because it will not overheat and become dry. Make sure the bowl does not touch the water.

Bake & store

With a few exceptions, most of the cookies in this book will keep well in a pan or airtight container and, in the case of bar cookies, even in the baking pan in which they were cooked, if it is kept covered with foil. However, the following tips will also help:

● Ideally, store baked cookies undecorated. Any item that is decorated with dairy products should be stored in the refrigerator.

● Store soft cookies separately from crisp varieties so that they don't all become soft.

● Store different flavored cookies separately so that their flavors do not mix.

● Only store cookies when they are completely cold. If stored while still warm, they are liable to stick together.

● One or two sugar cubes added to a container of cookies helps to keep them crisp.

● Most cookies can be frozen and thawed at short notice, but most are best when just baked.

The presentation

Finally, when serving your cookies, remember presentation makes all the difference. Serve the delicate types on fine china or glass plates, or use cake stands and baskets lined with napkins, or even pans lined with baking paper.

The beautifully photographed recipes in this book will capture your imagination—and with 200 of them to choose from you are really spoilt for choice!

1   *Chocolate chip cookies*

8 tbsp butter, softened, plus extra
    for greasing
heaping ½ cup dark brown sugar
1 egg
1¼ cups rolled oats
1 tbsp milk
1 tsp vanilla extract

1 cup all-purpose flour
1 tbsp unsweetened cocoa
½ tsp baking powder
6 oz/175 g semisweet chocolate,
    broken into pieces
6 oz/175 g milk chocolate,
    broken into pieces

Preheat the oven to 350°F/180°C. Grease 2 large baking sheets. Place the butter and sugar in a large bowl and beat together until light and fluffy. Beat in the egg, then add the oats, milk, and vanilla extract and beat together until well blended. Sift the flour, cocoa, and baking powder into the mixture and stir. Stir in the chocolate pieces.

Place tablespoonfuls of the mixture on the baking sheets and flatten slightly with a fork. Bake in the preheated oven for 15 minutes, or until slightly risen and firm.

Let cool on the baking sheets for 2 minutes, then transfer the cookies to wire racks to cool completely.

2   *White chocolate chip cookies*

Replace the semisweet and milk chocolate with 9¾ oz/275 g chopped white chocolate.

3   *Almond cookies with a cherry on top*

heaping ¾ cup butter, cut into cubes,
    plus extra for greasing
½ cup superfine sugar
½ tsp almond extract

2 cups self-rising flour
heaping ¼ cup ground almonds
25 candied cherries (total weight about
    4½ oz/125 g)

Preheat the oven to 350°F/180°C. Grease several large baking sheets. Place the butter in a large saucepan and heat gently until melted. Remove from the heat. Add the sugar and almond extract to the pan and stir together. Add the flour and ground almonds and mix to form a smooth dough.

Roll small pieces of the dough between your hands into smooth balls to make 25 in total. Place on the baking sheets, spaced well apart, and flatten slightly with your hands, then press a cherry gently into the center of each cookie. Bake in the preheated oven for 10–15 minutes, or until golden brown.

Let cool for 2–3 minutes on the baking sheets, then transfer the cookies to a wire rack to cool completely.

4 Cookies & cream sandwiches

9 tbsp butter, softened
⅔ cup confectioners' sugar
heaping ¾ cup all-purpose flour
½ cup unsweetened cocoa
½ tsp ground cinnamon

FILLING
4½ oz/125 g semisweet chocolate,
 broken into pieces
¼ cup heavy cream

Preheat the oven to 325°F/160°C. Line 2 large baking sheets with parchment paper. Place the butter and sugar in a large bowl and beat together until light and fluffy. Sift the flour, cocoa, and cinnamon into the mixture and mix to form a dough.

Place the dough between 2 sheets of parchment paper and roll out until the dough is ⅛ inch/3 mm thick. Cut out 2½-inch/6-cm rounds and place on the baking sheets. Bake in the preheated oven for 15 minutes, or until firm to the touch. Let cool for 2 minutes on the parchment paper, then transfer the cookies to wire racks to cool completely.

Meanwhile, make the filling. Place the chocolate and cream in a saucepan and heat gently until the chocolate has melted. Stir until smooth. Let cool, then chill in the refrigerator for 2 hours, or until firm. Sandwich the cookies together in pairs with a spoonful of the chocolate cream and serve.

5 With strawberry filling

Replace the semisweet chocolate with white chocolate, chop ½ cup dried strawberries into small pieces, and fold into the chilled filling.

6 Classic oatmeal cookies

¾ cup butter or margarine, plus extra
 for greasing
1⅓ cups raw brown sugar
1 egg
4 tbsp water

1 tsp vanilla extract
scant 4½ cups rolled oats
1 cup all-purpose flour
1 tsp salt
½ tsp baking soda

Preheat the oven to 180°C/350°F. Grease 2 large baking sheets. Place the butter and sugar in a large bowl and beat together until light and fluffy. Beat in the egg, water, and vanilla extract until the mixture is smooth. Mix the oats, flour, salt, and baking soda together in a separate bowl, then gradually stir the oat mixture into the creamed mixture until thoroughly combined.

Place tablespoonfuls of the dough onto the baking sheets, spaced well apart. Bake in the preheated oven for 15 minutes, or until golden brown. Transfer to a wire rack to cool completely.

7 Oatmeal & raisin cookies

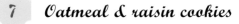

Add ½ cup chopped raisins to the dough mix.

1 cup butter, softened
¾ cup superfine sugar
1 egg yolk, lightly beaten
2 tsp vanilla extract
1⅓ cups all-purpose flour, plus extra
    for dusting

½ cup unsweetened cocoa
pinch of salt
7 oz/200 g white chocolate,
    broken into pieces
chocolate sprinkles, for decorating

Place the butter and sugar in a large bowl and mix well with a wooden spoon, then beat in the egg yolk and vanilla extract.

Sift together the flour, cocoa, and salt into the mixture and stir until thoroughly combined. Halve the dough, roll each piece into a ball, wrap in plastic wrap, and chill in the refrigerator for 30–60 minutes.

Preheat the oven to 375°F/190°C. Line 2 large baking sheets with parchment paper.

Unwrap the dough and roll out between 2 pieces of parchment paper to about ¼ inch/5 mm thick. Cut out 30 cookies with a 2½–2¾-inch/6–7-cm fluted round cutter and place them on the baking sheets, spaced well apart.

Bake in the preheated oven for 10–12 minutes. Let cool on the baking sheets for 5–10 minutes, then transfer the cookies to wire racks to cool completely.

Place the white chocolate in a heatproof bowl, set the bowl over a saucepan of gently simmering water, and heat until melted. Immediately remove from the heat and spread the melted chocolate over the cookies. Let cool slightly, then sprinkle with the chocolate sprinkles. Let cool and set before serving.

9 *Marbled cookies*

Omit the chocolate sprinkles and use 3½ oz/100 g melted semisweet chocolate to swirl into the white chocolate topping to create a marbled effect.

8 tbsp butter, cut into small pieces, plus
    extra for greasing
1¼ cups all-purpose flour, plus extra
    for dusting

pinch of salt
¼ cup superfine sugar, plus extra
    for sprinkling

Preheat the oven to 300°F/150°C. Grease a loose-bottom, 8-inch/20-cm round fluted tart pan with butter.

Place the flour, salt, and sugar in a large bowl and mix together. Add the butter and rub it into the dry ingredients. Continue to work the mixture until it forms a soft dough. Make sure you do not overwork the shortbread or it will be tough.

Lightly press the dough into the tart pan. If you don't have a fluted pan, roll out the dough on a lightly floured board, place on a baking sheet, and pinch the edges to form a scalloped pattern.

Using a knife, mark the dough into 8 pieces and prick all over with a fork. Bake in the preheated oven for 45–50 minutes, or until the shortbread is firm and just colored. Let cool for a few minutes in the pan, then sprinkle with sugar. Cut into portions and transfer to a wire rack to cool.

11 *Lemon & vanilla shortbread*

Split a vanilla bean in half lengthwise, carefully scrape out the seeds, and add to the flour along with the finely grated rind of 1 lemon.

¾ cup butter, softened
scant ½ cup confectioners' sugar,
     plus extra for dusting
1 small egg yolk

2½ tsp brandy
2¼ cups all-purpose flour
¼ tsp baking powder

Preheat the oven to 350°F/180°C. Line 2–3 large baking sheets with parchment paper.

Place the butter and confectioners' sugar in a large bowl and beat together until light and fluffy. Add the egg yolk and brandy and beat until the mixture is smooth. Sift the flour and baking powder into the mixture and beat until combined, then, using your hands, knead the dough until smooth.

Roll small pieces of the dough into smooth balls, then place them on the baking sheets, spaced well apart, and flatten slightly with your hands. Bake in the preheated oven for 15 minutes, or until firm to the touch and pale golden brown. Meanwhile, sift a layer of confectioners' sugar into a large roasting pan.

Let the shortbread cool for 2–3 minutes on the baking sheets, then place in the roasting pan in a single layer. Sift more confectioners' sugar generously over the top and let cool completely.

13   *Greek almond shortbread*

Use only 2 teaspoons of brandy and add ½ teaspoon of almond extract. Replace 1 cup of the flour with ground almonds.

14   *Greek pistachio shortbread*

Add ⅓ cup finely chopped pistachios to the mixture after adding the flour and baking powder.

15   *Greek lemon shortbread*

Add the finely grated rind of 1 lemon to the mixture with the egg yolk and replace the brandy with 2½ teaspoons of lemon juice.

8 tbsp unsalted butter, softened
¼ cup raw brown sugar
1 large egg, separated
½ tsp vanilla extract
1 cup all-purpose flour
pinch of salt

1 cup chopped mixed nuts
36 chocolate- or sugar-coated peanuts,
    for decorating

FROSTING
1 cup butter, softened
3 cups confectioners' sugar

Place the butter and sugar in a large bowl and beat together until light and fluffy. Stir in the egg yolk and vanilla extract and beat together, then add the flour and salt and beat to combine. Wrap the dough in plastic wrap and chill in the refrigerator for 3 hours.

Preheat the oven to 350°F/180°C. Line a large baking sheet with parchment paper.

Lightly whisk the egg white in a clean bowl and spread the chopped nuts out on a plate. Roll walnut-size pieces of the dough into balls. Dip each ball in the egg white, then roll in the nuts to coat and place on the baking sheet. Bake in the preheated oven for 5 minutes, then remove and make an indentation with your thumb in the middle of each cookie. Bake for an additional 5 minutes, then let the cookies cool completely on the baking sheet.

To make the buttercream, place the butter in a large bowl and beat until soft. Sift in the sugar and beat together until smooth. Spoon a little buttercream into the indentation of each cookie and top each one with 2 chocolate- or sugar-coated peanuts.

17 *With hazelnut & chocolate topping*

Replace the buttercream with 5 oz/140 g hazelnut chocolate spread.

¾ cup unsalted butter, softened,
    plus extra for greasing
1 cup superfine sugar
1 large egg, lightly beaten
1 tsp vanilla extract or almond extract
2¼ cups all-purpose flour, plus extra
    for dusting
pinch of salt

FOR DECORATING
1⅓ cups confectioners' sugar
about 1 tbsp cold water
yellow, pink, and blue food coloring
silver dragées
tubes of colored decorating icing

Place the butter and sugar in a large bowl and beat together until light and fluffy. Whisk the egg and vanilla together in a separate bowl, then beat into the butter mixture. Sift in the flour and salt and mix to form a dough. Wrap in plastic wrap and chill for 30 minutes.

Preheat the oven to 350°F/180°C. Grease a large baking sheet. Roll the dough out on a floured work surface to ¼ inch/5 mm thick. Cut out shapes with a flour-dipped, butterfly-shaped cookie cutter and place on the baking sheet. Bake in the preheated oven for 12–15 minutes, or until

they are golden brown. Let cool on wire racks.

To make the icing, sift the confectioners' sugar into a bowl, add the water, and mix until smooth. Divide the icing into portions and tint to pastel shades with food coloring. Spread the icing over the cookies and decorate with silver dragées. Let set, then finish decorating with decorating icing.

¾ cup unsalted butter, softened
½ cup light brown sugar
1 large egg, lightly beaten
1 tbsp honey
2 cups all-purpose flour, plus extra
   for dusting
½ tsp ground cinnamon

FOR DECORATING
1 cup confectioners' sugar
about ½ tsp cold water
3 tbsp chocolate sprinkles
20 gum drops
tubes of colored decorating icing

Place the butter and sugar in a large bowl and beat together until light and fluffy. Add the egg and honey and stir to combine. Sift in the flour and cinnamon and mix to form a soft dough. Wrap the dough in plastic wrap and chill in the refrigerator for 30 minutes.

Preheat the oven to 375°F/190°C. Line a large baking sheet with parchment paper. Cut the dough in half and roll in the remaining flour, then roll out each piece between 2 sheets of plastic wrap. Using a 2¾-inch/7-cm cookie cutter, cut out 10 disks from each piece and place on the baking sheet. Bake in the preheated oven for 10–12 minutes, or until golden brown. Let cool for 5 minutes, then transfer the cookies to a wire rack to cool completely.

Sift the confectioners' sugar into a bowl, add the water, and mix until smooth. Spread the cookies with a thin layer of icing, then use the chocolate sprinkles for hair and a gum drop for the nose. Let set, then draw in the eyes and mouth with the decorating icing.

20 *Fairy faces*

For fairy faces, ice the cookies according to the recipe but use 3 tablespoons of pink sprinkles for the hair and use pink decorating icing for the face.

9 tbsp unsalted butter, softened
⅔ cup superfine sugar
1 large egg yolk

¾ cup all-purpose flour
1 tsp ground cinnamon

Preheat the oven to 400°F/200°C. Line a large baking sheet with parchment paper.

Place the butter and 2 tablespoons of the sugar in a large bowl and beat together until light and fluffy. Add the egg yolk and mix together, then sift in the flour and mix to form a soft dough.

Mix the remaining sugar with the cinnamon. Take a teaspoon of dough and roll it in the sugar mixture. Place on the baking sheet and use a fork to press down until the cookie is ½ inch/1 cm thick. Repeat until all the dough is used up. Bake in the preheated oven for 10 minutes, or until golden brown. Let cool on a wire rack.

22 *Coconut buttery fork cookies*

Add 3½ oz/100 g shredded coconut to the dough and roll the cookies in the remaining superfine sugar, but omit the cinnamon.

1 cup butter, softened
¾ cup superfine sugar
1 egg yolk, lightly beaten
2 tsp passion fruit pulp
2 cups all-purpose flour
pinch of salt
½ cup dry unsweetened coconut

FOR DECORATING
1½ cups confectioners' sugar
1–1½ tbsp passion fruit pulp
edible silver glitter

Place the butter and sugar in a large bowl and beat together until light and fluffy then beat in the egg yolk and passion fruit pulp. Sift together the flour and salt into the mixture, add the coconut, and stir until thoroughly combined. Halve the dough, shape into balls, wrap in plastic wrap, and chill for 30–60 minutes.

Preheat the oven to 375°F/190°C. Line 2 baking sheets with parchment paper.

Unwrap the dough and roll out between 2 sheets of parchment paper. Cut out cookies with a 2¾-inch/7-cm angel-shaped cutter and place them on the baking sheets, spaced well apart.

Bake in the preheated oven for 10–15 minutes, or until light golden brown. Let cool for 5–10 minutes, then transfer to wire racks to cool completely.

Sift the confectioners' sugar into a bowl and stir in the passion fruit pulp until it is the consistency of thick cream. Leave the cookies on the racks and spread the icing over them. Sprinkle with the edible glitter and let set.

24 *Angel ornaments*

Before baking, make a hole with a metal skewer or straw in the top of each cookie. Check the holes are big enough when the cookies come out of the oven and pierce again if necessary. Cool and decorate as before. Using thin white ribbon, string chains of the angels together to hang on the Christmas tree.

1 cup butter, softened
¾ cup superfine sugar
finely grated rind of 1 lemon
1 egg yolk, lightly beaten
2 cups all-purpose flour
½ tsp ground cinnamon
pinch of salt
heaping ½ cup semisweet chocolate chips

FOR DECORATING
2 tbsp lightly beaten egg white
2 tbsp lemon juice
2 cups confectioners' sugar
30 silver dragées
food coloring pens

Place the butter, sugar, and lemon rind in a large bowl and beat together until light and fluffy, then beat in the egg yolk. Sift together the flour, cinnamon, and salt into the mixture, add the chocolate chips, and stir until thoroughly combined. Halve the dough, shape into balls, wrap in plastic wrap, and chill in the refrigerator for 30–60 minutes.

Preheat the oven to 375°F/190°C. Line 2 large baking sheets with parchment paper. Unwrap the dough and roll out between 2 sheets of parchment paper. Cut out cookies with a 2-inch/5-cm bell-shaped cutter and place them on the baking sheets, spaced well apart.

Bake in a preheated oven for 10–15 minutes, or until light golden brown. Let the cookies cool for 5–10 minutes, then transfer to wire racks to cool completely.

Mix the egg white and lemon juice together in a bowl, then gradually beat in the confectioners' sugar until smooth. Leave the cookies on the racks and spread the frosting over them. Place a silver dragée on the clapper shape at the bottom of the cookie and let set. When dry, use food coloring pens to draw patterns on the cookies.

26 *Colored bells*

Divide the frosting into 3 portions. Leave one white, color one portion with red food coloring, and the third with green and use to decorate the bells. Let set, then tie 3 cookies together in a stack, one of each color, using ribbon.

1 cup butter, softened
¾ cup superfine sugar
1 egg yolk, lightly beaten
2 tsp vanilla extract
2 cups all-purpose flour
pinch of salt

1 egg white, lightly beaten
2 tbsp colored sprinkles
14 oz/400 g fruit-flavored hard candies
    in different colors
25 lengths of ribbon, to hang

Place the butter and sugar into a bowl and beat together until light and fluffy, then beat in the egg yolk and vanilla extract. Sift together the flour and salt into the mixture and stir until combined. Halve the dough, shape into balls, wrap in plastic wrap, and chill in the refrigerator for 30–60 minutes.

Preheat the oven to 375°F/190°C. Line 2 large baking sheets with parchment paper. Unwrap the dough and roll out between 2 sheets of parchment paper. Cut out cookies with Christmas-themed cutters and place them on the baking sheets, spaced well apart.

Using the end of a large plain piping tip, cut out rounds from each shape and remove them. Make a small hole in the top of each cookie with a skewer so that they can be threaded with ribbon. Brush with egg white and sprinkle with colored sprinkles. Bake in the preheated oven for 7 minutes. Meanwhile, lightly crush the candies by tapping

them with a rolling pin. Unwrap and sort into separate bowls by color. Remove the cookies from the oven and fill the holes with the crushed candies. Return to the oven and bake for an additional 5–8 minutes, or until they are light golden brown and the candies have melted and filled the holes. Let cool on the baking sheets and then transfer to wire racks. Thread thin ribbon through the holes in the top and hang.

½ cup all-purpose flour, plus extra
    for dusting
1 tsp ground cinnamon
1 tsp ground ginger
6½ tbsp butter, cut into cubes
scant ½ cup light brown sugar
finely grated rind of 1 orange
1 egg, lightly beaten

FOR DECORATING
1¼ cups confectioners' sugar
3–4 tsp cold water
edible silver cake sparkles
silver dragées

Preheat the oven to 350°F/180°C. Line several large baking sheets with parchment paper.

Sift the flour, cinnamon, and ginger into a large bowl. Add the butter and rub it in with your fingertips until the mixture resembles fine breadcrumbs. Stir the sugar and orange rind into the mixture, add the egg, and mix together to form a soft dough.

Roll the dough out thinly to about ¼ inch/5 mm thick on a lightly floured work surface. Cut out shapes with a 2½-inch/6.5-cm snowflake- or star-shaped cutters and place on the baking sheets.

Bake in the preheated oven for 10–15 minutes, or until golden brown. Let cool on the baking sheets for 2–3 minutes, then transfer the cookies to a wire rack and let cool completely.

To make the icing, sift the confectioners' sugar into a large bowl and add enough water to make a smooth icing. Spread a little on each cookie, then sprinkle with sparkles and dragées.

29 *Easter animal cookies*

Use a rabbit-shaped cutter instead of a snowflake and add a raisin for the eyes. Alternatively, use a chick-shaped cutter and add a few drops of yellow food coloring to the icing.

1 cup butter, softened
¼ cup superfine sugar
1 egg yolk, lightly beaten
2 tsp vanilla extract
2 cups all-purpose flour

pinch of salt
1 tsp ground ginger
1 tbsp finely grated orange rind
1 tbsp unsweetened cocoa
1 egg white, lightly beaten

Place the butter and sugar in a large bowl and beat together until light and fluffy, then beat in the egg yolk and vanilla. Sift together the flour and salt into the mixture and stir until combined.

Divide the dough in half. Add the ginger and orange rind to one half and mix well. Shape the dough into a log 6 inches/15 cm long. Flatten the sides and top to square off the log to 2 inches/5 cm high. Wrap in plastic wrap and chill for 30–60 minutes.

Sift the cocoa into the other half of the dough and mix well.

Shape into a flattened log exactly the same size as the first one, wrap in plastic wrap, and chill in the refrigerator for 30–60 minutes.

Unwrap the dough and cut each log lengthwise into 3 slices. Cut each slice lengthwise into 3 strips. Brush the strips with egg white and stack them in threes, alternating the colors, so they are the same shape as the original logs. Wrap in plastic wrap and chill for 30–60 minutes.

Preheat the oven to 375°F/190°C. Line 2 large baking sheets with parchment paper.

Unwrap the logs and cut into slices with a sharp serrated knife, then place the cookies on the baking sheets, spaced well apart. Bake in the preheated oven for 12–15 minutes, or until firm. Let cool for 5–10 minutes, then transfer the cookies to wire racks to cool completely.

31 *Battenberg cookies*

Omit the orange rind and ginger. Use pink food coloring to tint one half of the dough and add cocoa to the other. Shape each dough portion into 2 logs and after chilling, cut each into 2 strips. Brush with egg white and stack a pink log on top of a chocolate one. Repeat and press the 4 pieces together into a rectangle. Wrap and chill. Cut into slices, then bake as before.

9 tbsp butter, softened, plus extra
    for greasing
heaping ½ cup chunky peanut butter
heaping 1 cup granulated sugar
1 egg, lightly beaten

heaping 1 cup all-purpose flour
½ tsp baking powder
pinch of salt
½ cup unsalted natural peanuts, chopped

Lightly grease 2 large baking sheets. Place the butter and peanut butter in a large bowl and beat together. Gradually add the sugar and beat together well. Add the egg, a little at a time, until it is combined. Sift the flour, baking powder, and salt into the peanut butter mixture. Add the peanuts and bring all of the ingredients together to form a soft dough. Wrap the dough in plastic wrap and chill for 30 minutes.

Preheat the oven to 375°F/190°C. Form the dough into 20 balls and place them on the baking sheets, about 2 inches/5 cm apart. Flatten them slightly with your hand.

Bake in the preheated oven for 15 minutes, or until golden brown. Let cool on wire racks.

1⅓ cups all-purpose flour, plus extra
   for dusting
heaping ⅔ cup butter, cut into small
   pieces, plus extra for greasing

scant ⅔ cup superfine sugar, plus extra
   for dusting
1 tsp vanilla extract

Preheat the oven to 350°F/180°C. Grease a large baking sheet. Sift the flour into a large bowl, add the butter, and rub it in with your fingertips until the mixture resembles fine breadcrumbs. Stir in the sugar and vanilla extract and mix together to form a firm dough.

Roll out the dough on a lightly floured work surface until it is ½ inch/1 cm thick. Cut out 12 hearts with a heart-shaped cookie cutter measuring about 2 inches/5 cm across and arrange the hearts on the baking sheet.

Bake in the preheated oven for 15–20 minutes, or until just colored. Transfer to a wire rack and let cool completely. Dust with a little superfine sugar just before serving.

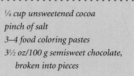

34 *With vanilla topping*

Beat 7 tablespoons of unsalted butter with the seeds from a vanilla bean, sift in 1⅓ cups confectioners' sugar, and beat until smooth. Spread over the hearts.

35 Sugared hearts
MAKES ABOUT 30

1 cup butter, softened
1½ cups superfine sugar
1 egg yolk, lightly beaten
2 tsp vanilla extract
heaping 1¾ cups all-purpose flour

¼ cup unsweetened cocoa
pinch of salt
3–4 food coloring pastes
3½ oz/100 g semisweet chocolate,
   broken into pieces

Place the butter and half the sugar in a large bowl and beat together until light and fluffy, then beat in the egg yolk and vanilla extract. Sift together the flour, cocoa, and salt into the mixture and stir until combined. Halve the dough, shape into balls, wrap in plastic wrap, and chill for 30–60 minutes.

Preheat the oven to 375°F/190°C. Line 2 large baking sheets with parchment paper. Unwrap the dough and roll out between 2 sheets of parchment paper. Cut out cookies with a heart-shaped cutter and place them on the baking sheets, spaced well apart. Bake in the preheated oven for 10–15 minutes, or until firm. Let cool on the baking sheets for 5–10 minutes, then transfer to wire racks to cool completely.

Meanwhile, divide the remaining sugar among 4 small plastic bags or bowls. Add a little food coloring paste to each and rub in until well mixed. Wear a plastic glove if mixing in bowls to prevent your hands from getting stained. Place the chocolate in a heatproof bowl, set the bowl over a saucepan of gently simmering water, and heat until melted. Let cool slightly.

Leave the cookies on the racks. Spread the melted chocolate over them and sprinkle with the colored sugar. Let set.

36 *White sugared hearts*

Replace the semisweet chocolate with white chocolate and sprinkle with dry unsweetened coconut instead of the colored sugar.

2 envelopes instant malted food drink
1 tbsp hot water
1 cup butter, softened
¾ cup superfine sugar
1 egg yolk, lightly beaten
2 cups all-purpose flour

pinch of salt
egg yolk and food coloring,
    for decorating

Place the malted drink in a bowl and stir in the hot, but not boiling water to make a paste.

Place the butter and sugar in a large bowl and beat together until light and fluffy, then beat in the egg yolk and malted drink paste. Sift together the flour and salt into the mixture and stir until thoroughly combined. Halve the dough, shape into balls, wrap in plastic wrap, and chill in the refrigerator for 30–60 minutes.

Preheat the oven to 375°F/190°C. Line 2 large baking sheets with parchment paper. Unwrap the dough and roll out between 2 sheets of parchment paper. Cut out cookies with a butterfly-shaped cutter and place them on the baking sheets.

Whisk an egg yolk and put a little of it in an egg cup. Add a few drops of food coloring and mix well. Using a fine paintbrush, paint a pattern on the butterflies' wings. Mix other colors with the beaten egg yolk in egg cups and add to the pattern.

Bake in the preheated oven for 10–15 minutes, or until firm. Let cool on the baking sheets for 5–10 minutes, then transfer the cookies to wire racks to cool completely.

1 cup butter, softened
¾ cup superfine sugar
1 egg yolk, lightly beaten
2 tsp vanilla extract
2 cups all-purpose flour, plus extra
    for dusting
pinch of salt
heaping 1 cup dry unsweetened
    coconut

FOR DECORATING
1½ tbsp lightly beaten egg white
1½ tbsp lemon juice
1½ cups confectioners' sugar
red, yellow, and green
    candied cherries
red and green gummy bears

Place the butter and sugar in a large bowl and beat together until light and fluffy, then beat in the egg yolk and vanilla extract. Sift together the flour and salt into the mixture, add the coconut, and stir until thoroughly combined. Halve the dough, roll each piece into a ball, wrap in plastic wrap, and chill for 30–60 minutes.

Preheat the oven to 375°F/190°C. Line 2 large baking sheets with parchment paper.

Roll out each piece of dough between 2 sheets of parchment paper to a rectangle about ¼ inch/5 mm thick. Using a sharp knife, cut the dough into bars about 4 x ¾ inches/10 x 2 cm in size and place them on the baking sheets, spaced well apart. Bake in the preheated oven for 10–12 minutes, or until golden brown. Let cool on the baking sheets for 5–10 minutes, then transfer the to wire racks to cool completely.

To make the frosting, mix the egg white and lemon juice together in a bowl, then gradually beat in the confectioners' sugar until smooth. Leave the cookies on the racks and spoon the frosting over them. Decorate some with a vertical row of red, yellow, and green candied cherries for traffic lights. For pedestrian lights, put a red gummy bear at the top of a cookie and a green one at the bottom. Let set.

39 *With jelly bean topping*

Instead of the frosting, place 5½ oz/150 g semisweet chocolate in a heatproof bowl, set the bowl over a saucepan of gently simmering water, and heat until melted. Spread the chocolate over the bars and press 3 jelly beans onto each.

Stained-glass window cookies

2½ cups all-purpose flour, plus extra
   for dusting
pinch of salt
1 tsp baking soda
7 tbsp unsalted butter
1 cup superfine sugar

1 large egg
1 tsp vanilla extract
4 tbsp dark corn syrup
50 mixed colored hard fruit candies
   (about 9 oz/250 g), chopped
25 lengths of ribbon, to hang

Sift the flour, salt, and baking soda into a large bowl, add the butter, and rub it in until the mixture resembles breadcrumbs. Stir in the sugar. Place the egg, vanilla extract, and corn syrup in a separate bowl and whisk together. Pour the egg into the flour mixture and mix to form a smooth dough. Wrap in plastic wrap and chill in the refrigerator for 30 minutes.

Preheat the oven to 350°F/ 180°C. Line 2 large baking sheets with parchment paper. Roll the dough out on a floured work surface to ¼ inch/5 mm thick. Use a variety of floured cookie cutters to cut out the cookies. Transfer them to the baking sheets and cut out shapes from the center of the cookies. Fill the holes with candies. Using a skewer, make a hole at the top of each cookie.

Bake in the preheated oven for 10–12 minutes, or until the candies are melted. Make sure the holes are still there, and pierce again if necessary. Let cool on the baking sheets until the centers have hardened. When cold, thread thin ribbon through the holes to hang up the cookies.

41 ## Mint window cookies

Cut all the cookies out with a round cookie cutter and use chopped, clear mint hard candies to fill the cavities. Hang using lengths of white ribbon.

Chocolate dominoes

1 cup butter, softened
¼ cup superfine sugar
1 egg yolk, lightly beaten
2 tsp vanilla extract
heaping 1¾ cups all-purpose flour
¼ cup unsweetened cocoa
pinch of salt
heaping ¼ cup dry unsweetened
   coconut
heaping ¼ cup white chocolate chips

Place the butter and sugar in a large bowl and beat together until light and fluffy, then beat in the egg yolk and vanilla extract. Sift together the flour, cocoa, and salt into the mixture, add the coconut, and stir until combined. Halve the dough, shape into balls, wrap in plastic wrap, and chill in the refrigerator for 30–60 minutes.

Preheat the oven to 375°F/ 190°C. Line 2 large baking sheets with parchment paper.

Unwrap the dough and roll out between 2 sheets of parchment paper. Cut out cookies with a 3½-inch/9-cm plain square cutter, then cut them in half to make rectangles. Place them on the baking sheets and, using a knife, make a line across the center of each without cutting through. Arrange the chocolate chips on top of the cookies to look like dominoes, pressing them in gently.

Bake in the preheated oven for 10–15 minutes, or until golden brown. Let cool for 5–10 minutes, then transfer to wire racks to cool completely.

43 ## With black icing

Sift 1 cup confectioners' sugar into a bowl and beat in 1 tablespoon of water until smooth. Add a few drops of black food coloring and mix until black. Use to ice the cookies, let set, then add the white dots with white decorating icing.

44 Double heart cookies

1 envelope instant latte
1½ tsp hot water
1 cup butter, softened
¾ cup superfine sugar
1 egg yolk, lightly beaten

heaping 1¼ cups all-purpose flour
1 tsp vanilla extract
3 tbsp unsweetened cocoa
pinch of salt

Place the instant latte into a small bowl and stir in the hot, but not boiling, water to make a paste.

Place the butter and sugar in a large bowl and beat together until light and fluffy, then beat in the egg yolk. Divide the mixture in half. Beat the latte paste into one half. Sift 1 cup of the flour with the salt into the mixture and stir until combined. Shape the dough into a ball, wrap in plastic wrap, and chill in the refrigerator for 30–60 minutes. Beat the vanilla extract into the other bowl, then sift together the remaining flour, the cocoa, and salt into the mixture. Stir until thoroughly combined. Shape the dough into a ball, wrap in plastic wrap, and chill for 30–60 minutes.

Preheat the oven to 375°F/190°C. Line 2 large baking sheets with parchment paper.

Unwrap both flavors of dough and roll out each between 2 sheets of parchment paper. Cut out cookies with a 2¾-inch/7-cm heart-shaped cutter and place them on the baking sheets, spaced well apart. Using a 1½–2-inch/4–5-cm/ heart-shaped cutter, cut out the centers of each larger heart and remove from the baking sheets. Place a small chocolate-flavored heart in the center of each large coffee-flavored heart and vice versa.

Bake in the preheated oven for 10–15 minutes. Let cool for 5–10 minutes, then transfer to wire racks to cool completely.

45 Pink hearts

Divide the dough into 3 portions and add pink food coloring to one portion, then make the cookies as before, contrasting the 3 different colored doughs.

46 Chocolate-dipped Viennese fingers

7 tbsp butter, plus extra for greasing
2 tbsp superfine sugar
½ tsp vanilla extract

¾ cup self-rising flour
3½ oz/100 g semisweet chocolate

Preheat the oven to 325°F/160°C. Grease 2 large baking sheets. Place the butter, sugar, and vanilla extract in a large bowl and beat together until light and fluffy. Stir in the flour, mixing evenly to make a fairly stiff dough.

Place the mixture in a pastry bag fitted with a large star tip and pipe about 16 fingers, each 2½ inches/6 cm long, onto the baking sheets. Bake in the preheated oven for 10–15 minutes, or until pale golden. Let cool on the baking sheets for 2–3 minutes, then transfer to a wire rack to cool completely.

Place the chocolate in a small heatproof bowl, set over a saucepan of gently simmering water, and heat until melted. Remove from the heat. Dip the ends of each cookie into the chocolate to coat, then place on a sheet of parchment paper and let set.

47 Viennese pinks

Omit the chocolate and dip each end of the fingers into pink frosting made by beating 1 cup sifted confectioners' sugar with 1 tablespoon of water and a drop of pink food coloring. Before the frosting is dry, dip the tips into pink sprinkles, then let set.

1 cup butter, softened
¾ cup superfine sugar
1 egg yolk, lightly beaten
2 tsp grenadine
2 cups all-purpose flour

pinch of salt
5–6 tbsp unsalted dried pomegranate
seeds or roasted melon seeds

Place the butter and sugar in a large bowl and beat together until light and fluffy, then beat in the egg yolk and grenadine. Sift together the flour and salt into the mixture and stir until combined. Halve the dough, shape into balls, wrap in plastic wrap, and chill in the refrigerator for 30–60 minutes.

Preheat the oven to 375°F/190°C. Line 2 large baking sheets with parchment paper.

Unwrap the dough and roll out between 2 sheets of parchment paper to about ⅛ inch/3 mm thick. Sprinkle half the seeds over each piece of dough and lightly roll the rolling pin over them. Cut out letters with alphabet cutters and place them on the baking sheets, spaced well apart.

Bake in the preheated oven for 10–12 minutes, or until golden brown. Let cool on the baking sheets for 5–10 minutes, then transfer the cookies to wire racks to cool completely.

49 *Tutti frutti cookies*

Replace the seeds with 1 oz/25 g each of chopped candied fruit, candied cherries, and angelica and add to the cookie dough.

1 cup butter, softened
¾ cup superfine sugar
1 egg yolk, lightly beaten
½ tsp vanilla extract
2 cups all-purpose flour
pinch of salt

FOR DECORATING
1¼ cups confectioners' sugar
1–2 tbsp warm water
food colorings
silver and gold dragées
colored sprinkles
dry unsweetened coconut
sugar sprinkles
sugar stars, hearts, and flowers

Place the butter and sugar in a large bowl and beat together until light and fluffy, then beat in the egg yolk and vanilla extract. Sift together the flour and salt into the mixture and stir until thoroughly combined. Halve the dough, shape into balls, wrap in plastic wrap, and chill for 30–60 minutes.

Preheat the oven to 375°F/ 190°C. Line 2 large baking sheets with parchment paper.

Unwrap the dough and roll out between 2 sheets of parchment paper to about ⅛ inch/3 mm thick. Cut out cookies with a star-shaped cutter and place them on the baking sheets, spaced well apart. Bake in the preheated oven for 10–15 minutes, or until light golden brown. Let cool on the baking sheets for 5–10 minutes, then transfer to wire racks to cool completely.

To decorate, sift the confectioners' sugar into a bowl and stir in enough warm water until it is the consistency of thick cream. Divide the icing among 3–4 bowls and add a few drops of your chosen food colorings to each. Leave the cookies on the racks and spread the different colored icings over them to the edges. Arrange silver and gold dragées on top and/or sprinkle with colored sprinkles and sugar shapes. If you like, color dry unsweetened coconut with food coloring in a contrasting color and sprinkle on top. Let the cookies set.

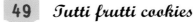

51 *Marzipan stars*

Omit the icing and thinly roll 5½ oz/150 g white marzipan out on a work surface dusted with confectioners' sugar. Cut out 30 stars with the star-shaped cutter and use a little beaten egg white to secure the marzipan to the cookies, then use a kitchen blow torch to toast the edges of the marzipan.

9 tbsp butter, softened
1 cup superfine sugar
1 egg, lightly beaten
½ tsp vanilla extract
1 cup all-purpose flour
⅓ cup unsweetened cocoa
½ tsp baking soda

Preheat the oven to 350°F/180°C. Line several large baking sheets with parchment paper.

Place the butter and sugar in a large bowl and beat together until light and fluffy. Add the egg and vanilla extract and mix until smooth. Sift in the flour, cocoa, and baking soda and beat until well mixed.

With dampened hands, roll walnut-size pieces of the dough into smooth balls. Place on the baking sheets, spaced well apart.

Bake in the preheated oven for 10–12 minutes, or until set. Let cool on the baking sheets for 5 minutes, then transfer the cookies to wire racks to cool completely before serving.

53 *With chocolate topping*

As the cookies cool, place 2¾ oz/75 g semisweet chocolate in a heatproof bowl, set the bowl over a saucepan of gently simmering water, and heat until melted. Remove from the heat and stir until smooth. Spoon the chocolate into a pastry bag fitted with a writing tip and drizzle the chocolate over the cookies in a decorative zigzag pattern, then let set.

54 *Sugar-coated midnight cookies*

Sprinkle ¼ cup granulated sugar on a large plate. Roll each ball of dough in the sugar to coat before placing on the baking sheets.

3½ cups all-purpose flour, plus extra
    for dusting
2 tsp baking powder
1 cup butter, cut into cubes, plus extra
    for greasing

1¾ cups superfine sugar
2 large eggs, lightly beaten
2 tsp vanilla extract

Sift the flour and baking powder into a large bowl. Add the butter and rub it in with your fingertips until the mixture resembles fine breadcrumbs. Stir the sugar into the mixture, add the eggs and vanilla extract, and mix together to form a soft dough.

Turn the mixture onto a lightly floured work surface and divide the dough in half. Shape each piece of dough into a log shape about 2½ inches/6 cm thick. Wrap each log in parchment paper and then in foil and chill in the refrigerator for at least 8 hours, or until required.

Preheat the oven to 375°F/190°C. Grease several large baking sheets. Slice the dough into as many ⅜-inch/8-mm slices as required and place on the baking sheets, spaced well apart. Return any remaining dough to the refrigerator for up to 1 week, or to the freezer until required. Bake in the preheated oven for 10–15 minutes, or until golden brown. Leave on the baking sheet to cool slightly for 2–3 minutes, then transfer the cookies to a wire rack to cool completely.

 56 *Cherry refrigerator cookies*

Finely chop ⅔ cup candied cherries and add to the mixture with the superfine sugar.

 57 *Chocolate refrigerator cookies*

Finely grate 3½ oz/100 g semisweet chocolate and add to the mixture with the superfine sugar.

 58 *Coconut refrigerator cookies*

Add heaping 1 cup dry unsweetened coconut with the superfine sugar.

 59 *Dried fruit refrigerator cookies*

Finely chop heaping ½ cup golden raisins, raisins, or cranberries and add to the mixture with the superfine sugar.

 60 *Ginger refrigerator cookies*

Omit the vanilla extract and sift 3 teaspoons of ground ginger into the mixture with the flour.

 61 *Lemon refrigerator cookies*

Omit the vanilla extract and finely grate the rind of 2 lemons into the mixture with the superfine sugar.

62 *Orange refrigerator cookies*

Omit the vanilla extract and finely grate the rind of 2 oranges into the mixture with the superfine sugar.

 **63** *Spicy refrigerator cookies*

Omit the vanilla extract and sift 4 teaspoons of apple pie spice into the mixture with the flour.

64 *Walnut refrigerator cookies*

Chop 1 cup walnut halves and add to the mixture with the superfine sugar.

heaping 1 cup unsalted
butter, softened
1⅓ cups superfine sugar
2 large eggs, lightly beaten
3¼ cups all-purpose flour, plus extra
for dusting
2 tsp baking powder
pinch of salt
few drops of food coloring
tube of decorating icing

Place the butter and sugar in a large bowl and beat together until light and fluffy. Gradually add the eggs and beat to combine, then sift in the flour, baking powder, and salt and mix to form a dough. Wrap the dough in plastic wrap and chill in the refrigerator for 2 hours.

Preheat the oven to 325°F/ 160°C. Line 2 large baking sheets with parchment paper.

Set aside one third of the dough and leave uncolored. Divide the remaining dough into portions and knead in different food colorings. Shape the dough into animal shapes (see right) and place the cookies on the baking sheets. Bake for 20–25 minutes. Let cool on a wire rack. Add eyes and other features with the decorating icing.

Cow cookie: Shape an oval piece of colored dough to 2½ inches/6 cm across for the body. Roll another piece of dough into a log 2½ inches/6 cm long and ½ inch/1 cm wide, then cut into 3 equal pieces—use 2 for the legs and 1 for the head. Roll uncolored dough into small circles and use as the udder, nose, and markings. Make a thin tail. Press the pieces well together.

Pig cookie: Shape an oval piece of colored dough to 2½ inches/6 cm across for the body; flatten. Shape a smaller oval piece to 1¼ inches/3 cm for the head; flatten. Use uncolored dough for the snout, ears, and tail.

Fluffy sheep cookie: For the body, roll small balls of uncolored dough and lay them on the baking sheet, touching each other in an oval shape. Use colored dough to shape the head and feet.

7 tbsp butter
½ cup light brown sugar
1 tbsp dark corn syrup

heaping 1 cup self-rising flour
3 oz/85 g sugar-coated chocolates

Preheat the oven to 350°F/180°C. Line several large baking sheets with parchment paper. Place the butter and sugar in a large bowl and whisk together until pale and creamy, then whisk the dark corn syrup into the mixture until smooth. Add ½ cup flour and whisk together until mixed. Stir in the sugar-coated chocolates and remaining flour then, with your hands, knead the mixture until smooth.

Roll small pieces of the dough between your hands into smooth balls to make 15 cookies in total and place them on the baking sheets, spacing them well apart. Bake in the preheated oven for 10–15 minutes, or until golden brown.

Leave on the baking sheets for 2–3 minutes, then transfer the cookies to a wire rack and let cool completely.

1 cup butter, softened
¾ cup superfine sugar
1 egg yolk, lightly beaten
1 tsp peppermint extract
2 cups all-purpose flour
pinch of salt
heaping 1 cup dry unsweetened coconut

FOR DECORATING
3½ oz/100 g white chocolate,
　broken into pieces
3½ oz/100 g milk chocolate,
　broken into pieces

Place the butter and sugar in a large bowl and beat together until light and fluffy, then beat in the egg yolk and peppermint extract. Sift together the flour and salt into the mixture, add the coconut, and stir until combined. Divide the mixture in half, shape into balls, wrap in plastic wrap, and chill for 30–60 minutes.

Preheat the oven to 375°F/190°C. Line 2 large baking sheets with parchment paper. Unwrap the dough and roll out between 2 sheets of parchment paper to about ⅛ inch/3 mm thick.

Cut out stars with a 2½–2¾-inch/6–7-cm cutter and place them on the baking sheets, spaced well apart.

Bake in the preheated oven for 10–12 minutes, or until light golden. Let cool on the baking sheets for 5–10 minutes, then transfer the cookies to wire racks to cool completely.

Place the white chocolate and the milk chocolate in separate heatproof bowls, set the bowls over 2 saucepans of gently simmering water, and heat until melted. Leave the cooled cookies on the racks and drizzle first with melted white chocolate and then with melted milk chocolate, using a teaspoon. Let set.

68 *White mint stars*

Omit the milk chocolate and melt 7 oz/200 g white chocolate in a heatproof bowl set over a pan of gently simmering water. Spread to cover each cookie and sprinkle over chocolate sprinkles.

pinch of salt
30 yellow marshmallows,
    halved horizontally
10½ oz/300 g semisweet chocolate,
    broken into pieces
4 tbsp orange marmalade
15 walnut halves, for decorating

2 tsp finely grated orange rind
1 egg yolk, lightly beaten
1¾ cups all-purpose flour
¼ cup unsweetened cocoa
½ tsp ground cinnamon

Place the butter, sugar, and orange rind in a large bowl and beat together until light and fluffy, then beat in the egg yolk. Sift together the flour, cocoa, cinnamon, and salt into the mixture and stir until combined. Halve the dough, shape into balls, wrap in plastic wrap, and chill for 30–60 minutes.

Preheat the oven to 375°F/190°C. Line 2 large baking sheets with parchment paper. Unwrap the dough and roll out between

2 sheets of parchment paper. Cut out cookies with a 2½-inch/6-cm fluted round cutter and place them on the baking sheets, spaced well apart. Bake in the preheated oven for 10–15 minutes. Let cool for 5 minutes. Turn half the cookies upside down and put 4 marshmallow halves on each. Bake for an additional 1–2 minutes. Let the cookies stand on wire racks for 30 minutes.

Place the chocolate in a heatproof bowl, set the bowl over a saucepan of gently simmering water, and heat until melted. Let cool.

Line a baking sheet with parchment paper. Spread the marmalade over the undersides of the uncovered cookies and place them on top of the marshmallow-covered cookies. Dip the cookies in the melted chocolate to coat, letting the excess drip back into the bowl, then place them on the baking sheet. Place a walnut half in the center of each cookie and let set.

70 White s'mores

Replace the semisweet chocolate with white chocolate. Scatter over ⅔ cup shelled, chopped pistachios to replace the walnuts.

71 Thanksgiving cookies

1 cup butter, softened
¾ cup superfine sugar
1 egg yolk, lightly beaten
2 tsp orange juice
2 cups all-purpose flour

pinch of salt
heaping ⅓ cup fresh or dried blueberries
heaping ½ cup fresh or dried cranberries
⅓ cup white chocolate chips

Preheat the oven to 375°F/190°C. Line 2 large baking sheets with parchment paper. Place the butter and sugar in a large bowl and beat together until light and fluffy, then beat in the egg yolk and orange juice. Sift together the flour and salt into the mixture, then add the blueberries, cranberries, and chocolate chips and stir until combined.

Scoop up tablespoons of the dough and place them on the baking sheets, spaced well apart. Bake in the preheated oven for 10–15 minutes, or until light golden brown.

Let cool on the baking sheets for 5–10 minutes, then transfer the cookies to wire racks to cool completely.

72 Cherry Thanksgiving cookies

Replace the blueberries and cranberries with heaping ½ cup chopped, dried cherries. Replace the white chocolate chips with semisweet chocolate chips.

Dinosaur cookies

1 cup unsalted butter, softened
1 cup smooth peanut butter
1 cup granulated sugar
1 cup light brown sugar
2 tsp baking powder
¼ tsp salt

2 large eggs
1 tsp vanilla extract
2 cups all-purpose flour, plus extra
   for dusting
silver dragées and tube of green
   decorating icing, for decorating

Place the butter and peanut butter in a large bowl and beat together until smooth. Add the sugars, baking powder, and salt and beat well to combine. Whisk the eggs and vanilla extract together in a separate bowl, then add to the mixture and mix well. Sift in the flour and mix to form a smooth dough. Wrap in plastic wrap and chill for 30 minutes.

Preheat the oven to 350°F/180°C. Roll the dough out on a floured work surface and cut out shapes with dinosaur cookie cutters dipped in flour. Re-roll any trimmings and cut out more cookies. Press silver dragées into the dough for eyes and place on 2 large nonstick baking sheets. Bake in the preheated oven for 10–12 minutes.

Let cool for 2 minutes, then transfer to a wire rack to cool completely. Decorate the dinosaurs with green decorating icing.

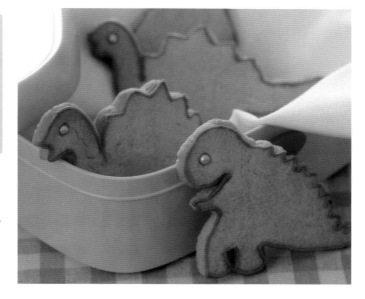

74 *Chocolate dinosaur cookies*

Add 3 teaspoons of cocoa to the dough and knead in before chilling.

Bedtime bears

8 tbsp unsalted butter, softened
½ cup superfine sugar
1 tsp baking powder
pinch of salt
1 large egg, lightly beaten
1 tsp milk

1 tsp vanilla extract
¼ cup unsweetened cocoa, plus extra
   for dusting
1 cup all-purpose flour
25 cookie bears, 2¼-inch/7-cm tall
3 tbsp smooth peanut butter

Place the butter and sugar in a large bowl and beat together until light and fluffy. Add the baking powder, salt, egg, milk, and vanilla extract and beat well. Sift in the cocoa and flour and mix to form a smooth dough. Wrap in plastic wrap and chill in the refrigerator for 3 hours.

Preheat the oven to 350°F/180°C. Roll the dough out on a work surface dusted with cocoa, then cut into twenty-five 2-inch/5-cm squares. Place a cookie bear diagonally on the square and secure with peanut butter. Fold up the bottom and sides of the dough to form a blanket around the bear, leaving the top third of the bear exposed. Press to secure and place on a large nonstick baking sheet. Bake in the preheated oven for 10 minutes. Cool on a wire rack.

76 *With colored blankets*

Omit the cocoa and divide the dough into portions. Tint each portion with a few drops of different food coloring. Roll out and cut as usual, and wrap the cookie bears in the colored dough blankets.

Ultimate iced sugar cutouts

6 tbsp unsalted butter, softened
½ cup superfine sugar
2 large eggs
½ tsp vanilla extract
scant 1½ cups all-purpose flour,
    plus extra for dusting

1 tsp baking powder
pinch of salt

ICING
1⅓ cups confectioners' sugar
about 1 tbsp cold water
few drops of food coloring

Place the butter and sugar in a large bowl and beat together until light and fluffy. Whisk the eggs and vanilla extract in another bowl, then add to the butter and sugar mixture. Sift in the flour, baking powder, and salt and beat together to form a dough. Wrap in plastic wrap and chill in the refrigerator for 1 hour.

Preheat the oven to 350°F/180°C. Line 2 large baking sheets with parchment paper. Roll the dough out on a floured work surface to about ¼ inch/5 mm thick. Cut out cookies with a variety of cookie cutter shapes dipped in flour. Place them on the baking sheets. Bake in the preheated oven for 10–12 minutes, or until golden brown. Let cool on wire racks.

Sift the confectioners' sugar into a bowl and mix with the water until smooth. Color the frosting as desired and spread over the cooled cookies, then let set.

78 Chocolate orange cookies

7 tbsp butter, softened
⅓ cup superfine sugar
1 egg
1 tbsp milk
2 cups all-purpose flour, plus extra
    for dusting
2 tbsp unsweetened cocoa

ICING
1½ cups confectioners' sugar
3 tbsp orange juice
a little semisweet chocolate, broken
    into pieces

Preheat the oven to 350°F/180°C. Line 2 large baking sheets with sheets of wax paper. Place the butter and sugar in a large bowl and beat together until light and fluffy. Beat in the egg and milk until thoroughly combined. Sift the flour and cocoa into the bowl and gradually mix together to form a soft dough.

Roll out the dough on a lightly floured work surface until it is about ¼ inch/5 mm thick. Cut out rounds with a 2-inch/5-cm fluted round cookie cutter and place them on the baking sheets. Bake in the preheated oven for 10–12 minutes, or until golden. Let cool on the baking sheet for a few minutes, then transfer the cookies to a wire rack to cool completely and become crisp.

To make the icing, sift the confectioners' sugar in a bowl and stir in enough orange juice to form a thin icing that will coat the back of the spoon. Place a spoonful of icing in the center of each cookie and let set.

Place the semisweet chocolate in a heatproof bowl, set the bowl over a saucepan of gently simmering water, and heat until melted. Drizzle thin lines of melted chocolate over the cookies and let set before serving.

79 With coffee icing

Replace the orange juice in the frosting with 2–3 tablespoons of cold, strong espresso coffee.

80 *Lemon & lime cookies*

5 oz/140 g semisweet chocolate, broken
    into pieces, for decorating
30 thinly pared strips of lime rind,
    for decorating
1 cup butter, softened
¼ cup superfine sugar
1 egg yolk, lightly beaten
2 tsp lime juice

2 cups all-purpose flour
pinch of salt
finely grated rind of 1 lemon

ICING
1 tbsp lightly beaten egg white
1 tbsp lime juice
1 cup confectioners' sugar

To make the decoration, place the chocolate in a heatproof bowl, set the bowl over a saucepan of gently simmering water, and heat until melted. Let cool slightly. Line a baking sheet with parchment paper. Dip the strips of lime rind into the chocolate until coated, then put on the baking sheet to set.

Place the butter and sugar in a large bowl and beat together until light and fluffy, then beat in the egg yolk and lime juice. Sift together the flour and salt into the mixture, add the lemon rind, and stir until combined. Halve the dough, shape into balls, wrap in plastic wrap, and chill in the refrigerator for 30–60 minutes.

Preheat the oven to 375°F/190°C. Line 2 large baking sheets with parchment paper. Unwrap the dough and roll out between 2 sheets of parchment paper to about ⅛ inch/3 mm thick. Cut out rounds with a 2½-inch/6-cm plain cutter and place them on the baking sheets. Bake in the preheated oven for 10–15 minutes, or until golden brown. Let cool on the baking sheets for 5–10 minutes, then transfer to wire racks to cool completely.

To make the icing, place the egg white and lime juice in a bowl and mix together, then gradually beat in the confectioners' sugar until smooth. Ice the cookies and top with the chocolate-coated lime rind. Let set.

81 *With semisweet chocolate topping*

Omit the lime rind and simply drizzle the melted semisweet chocolate over the icing and let set.

82 *Lemon & sesame seed cookies*

2 tbsp sesame seeds
1 cup butter, softened
¼ cup superfine sugar
1 tbsp finely grated lemon rind
1 egg yolk, lightly beaten
2 cups all-purpose flour
pinch of salt

ICING
1 cup confectioners' sugar
few drops of lemon extract
1 tbsp hot water

Dry-roast the sesame seeds in a heavy-bottom skillet over low heat, stirring frequently, for 2–3 minutes, or until they give off their aroma. Let cool.

Place the butter, sugar, lemon rind, and toasted seeds in a large bowl and beat together until light and fluffy, then beat in the egg yolk. Sift together the flour and salt into the mixture and stir until combined. Halve the dough, form it into balls, wrap in plastic wrap, and chill in the refrigerator for 30–60 minutes.

Preheat the oven to 375°F/190°C. Line 2 large baking sheets with parchment paper. Unwrap the dough and roll out between 2 sheets of parchment paper. Cut out rounds with a 2½-inch/6-cm cutter and place them on the baking sheets, spaced well apart. Bake in the preheated oven for 10–12 minutes, or until light golden brown. Let cool on the baking sheets for 5–10 minutes, then transfer the cookies to wire racks to cool completely.

To make the icing, sift the confectioners' sugar into a bowl, add the lemon extract, and gradually stir in the hot water until the icing is smooth and has the consistency of thick cream. Leave the cooled cookies on the racks and spread the frosting over them. Let set.

83 *Lime & sesame seed cookies*

Omit the lemon in this recipe and replace with lime, then top the icing with finely grated lime rind.

~~rshmallow daisies~~

¾ cup superfine sugar
1 egg yolk, lightly beaten
2 tsp vanilla extract
1⅔ cups all-purpose flour
½ cup unsweetened cocoa

pinch of salt
about 90 white mini marshmallows,
    halved horizontally
4 tbsp peach jam
4 tbsp yellow sugar sprinkles

Place the butter and sugar in a large bowl and beat together until light and fluffy, then beat in the egg yolk and vanilla extract.

Sift together the flour, cocoa, and salt into the mixture and stir until thoroughly combined. Halve the dough, roll each piece into a ball, wrap in plastic wrap, and chill in the refrigerator for 30–60 minutes.

Preheat the oven to 375°F/ 190°C. Line 2 large baking sheets with parchment paper.

Unwrap the dough and roll out between 2 sheets of parchment paper to about ½ inch/1 cm thick. Cut out 30 cookies with a 2-inch/ 5-cm flower cookie cutter and put them on the baking sheets, making sure they are spaced well apart.

Bake in the preheated oven for 10–12 minutes, or until firm. Remove from the oven but do not turn off the heat. Arrange the marshmallow pieces over the petals of the flowers, cutting them to fit if necessary. Return to the oven for 30–60 seconds, or until the marshmallows have softened.

Let cool on the baking sheets for 5–10 minutes, then transfer the cookies to wire racks to cool completely. Meanwhile, heat the jam in a small saucepan, strain into a bowl, and let cool. Pipe a small circle of jam in the center of each flower and top with the sugar sprinkles.

85 Chocolate daisies

Omit the cocoa from the dough mixture and use small chocolate disks instead of the marshmallows.

86 Chocolate florentines

3½ tbsp unsalted butter
4 tbsp superfine sugar
1 tbsp dark corn syrup
heaping ⅓ cup all-purpose flour

scant ¼ cup candied cherries, chopped
½ cup slivered almonds
heaping ¼ cup candied peel, chopped
6 oz/175 g semisweet chocolate, chopped

Preheat the oven to 350°F/180°C. Line 2 large baking sheets with parchment paper. Heat the butter, sugar, and corn syrup together in a saucepan over low heat until the butter is melted and the sugar is dissolved. Stir in the flour, cherries, almonds, and candied peel.

Make the florentines in batches. Place heaped teaspoons of the mixture on the baking sheets, spaced well apart, and flatten slightly with the back of a spoon. Bake in the preheated oven for 8–10 minutes, or until golden brown. Let cool on the baking sheets for 2–3 minutes, then transfer to a wire rack and leave until cold. Repeat until you have 20 florentines.

Place the chocolate in a heatproof bowl, set the bowl over a saucepan of gently simmering water, and heat until melted. Using a pastry brush, spread the chocolate over the bottom of each florentine and place chocolate-side up on a wire rack to cool and set.

87 Ginger florentines

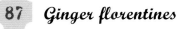

Replace the candied cherries and candied peel with 3 oz/85 g chopped crystallized ginger.

7 tbsp unsalted butter, softened
¼ cup superfine sugar
heaping ⅓ cup cornstarch
¾ cup all-purpose flour, plus 1 tbsp
    for dusting

1 large egg yolk
1 tbsp milk
2 tbsp unsweetened cocoa

Place the butter and sugar in a large bowl and beat together until light and fluffy. Sift in the cornstarch and the flour and mix well to combine, then add the egg yolk and a little milk to form a stiff dough.

Divide the dough mixture in half, add the cocoa to one half, and mix well together. Wrap both doughs in plastic wrap and chill in the refrigerator for 30 minutes.

Roll each piece of dough into a rectangle ⅛ inch/3 mm thick. Lay the chocolate dough on top of the white dough, then press together and trim the edges. Roll up lengthwise, wrap tightly in plastic wrap, and chill in the refrigerator for 30 minutes.

Preheat the oven to 350°F/ 180°C. Unwrap the dough and cut across the roll into 20 slices, then place the cookies on a nonstick baking sheet. Bake in the preheated oven for 15–20 minutes. Let cool on a wire rack.

89 *Hazelnut whirly pinwheel cookies*

Add 3 tablespoons of finely chopped hazelnuts to the chocolate dough and knead in before chilling the dough.

90 *Good-for-you wholemeal cookies*   MAKES 36

2¼ cups whole wheat flour, plus extra
    for dusting
2 tbsp wheat germ
¼ tsp baking soda
½ tsp salt

¼ cup superfine sugar
9 tbsp unsalted butter, cubed
1 large egg, lightly beaten
1 tsp vanilla extract

Preheat the oven to 325°F/170°C. Place the flour, wheat germ, baking soda, salt, and sugar in a large bowl and stir together until combined. Add the butter and rub it in until the mixture resembles breadcrumbs.

Whisk the egg and vanilla extract in a separate bowl and add to the mixture, adding a little cold water if needed to bring the dough together. Roll the dough out on a floured board. Use a 2¾-inch/7-cm floured cookie cutter to cut out the cookies and place them on nonstick baking sheets, re-rolling the dough when necessary.

Bake in batches in the preheated oven for 20–25 minutes, or until dry but not brown. Let cool on a wire rack.

91 *Fruit wholemeal cookies*

Knead 2 tablespoons of chopped raisins or chopped candied peel and ½ teaspoon of apple pie spice into the dough before rolling out.

Oaty raisin & hazelnut cookies

⅓ cup raisins, chopped
½ cup orange juice
1 cup butter, softened
¾ cup superfine sugar
1 egg yolk, lightly beaten
2 tsp vanilla extract

1⅔ cups all-purpose flour
pinch of salt
⅔ cup rolled oats
⅓ cup hazelnuts, chopped
about 30 whole hazelnuts

Preheat the oven to 375°F/190°C. Line 2 large baking sheets with parchment paper. Place the raisins in a bowl, add the orange juice, and let soak for 10 minutes.

Place the butter and sugar in a large bowl and beat together until light and fluffy, then beat in the egg yolk and vanilla extract. Sift together the flour and salt into the mixture and add the oats and hazelnuts. Drain the raisins, add them to the mixture, and stir until combined. Scoop up tablespoons of the mixture and place them in mounds on the baking sheets, spaced well apart. Flatten slightly and place a whole hazelnut in the center of each cookie.

Bake in the preheated oven for 12–15 minutes, or until golden brown. Let cool on the baking sheets for 5–10 minutes, then transfer to wire racks to cool completely.

93 *Oaty golden raisin & walnut cookies*

Replace the raisins and hazelnuts with ⅓ cup chopped golden raisins and ⅔ cup chopped walnuts.

94 *Lemon cornmeal cookies*

7 tbsp butter, softened
⅓ cup superfine sugar
2 large eggs, lightly beaten
finely grated rind of 1 lemon
1 tbsp lemon juice

1 cup all-purpose flour
½ cup cornmeal
12 whole blanched almonds

Preheat the oven to 375°F/190°C. Line several large baking sheets with parchment paper. Place the butter and sugar in a large bowl and whisk until pale and creamy. Whisk the beaten eggs, lemon rind, and juice into the mixture until smooth, then add the flour and cornmeal and beat together until mixed.

Place the mixture in a pastry bag fitted with a plain ¾-inch/2-cm tip. Pipe swirls, measuring about 2½ inches/6 cm in diameter, onto the baking sheets, spaced well apart, and top each cookie with a blanched almond.

Bake in the preheated oven for 10–15 minutes, or until lightly golden brown. Let cool on the baking sheets for 5 minutes, then transfer the cookies to a wire rack to cool completely.

Orange & chocolate fingers

1 cup butter, softened
¼ cup superfine sugar
finely grated rind of 1 orange
1 egg yolk, lightly beaten
2 tsp orange juice

2 cups all-purpose flour
1 tsp ground ginger
pinch of salt
4 oz/115 g semisweet chocolate,
    broken into pieces

Place the butter, sugar, and orange rind in a large bowl and beat together until light and fluffy, then beat in the egg yolk and orange juice. Sift together the flour, ginger, and salt into the mixture and stir until combined. Shape the dough into a ball, wrap in plastic wrap, and chill in the refrigerator for 30–60 minutes.

Preheat the oven to 375°F/190°C. Line 2 large baking sheets with parchment paper. Unwrap the dough and roll out between 2 sheets of parchment paper to a rectangle. Using a sharp knife, cut it into 4 x ¾-inch/10 x 2-cm strips and place them on the baking sheets, spaced well apart.

Bake in the preheated oven for 10–12 minutes, or until light golden brown. Let cool for 5–10 minutes, then transfer to wire racks to cool completely.

Place the chocolate in a heatproof bowl, set the bowl over a saucepan of gently simmering water, and heat until melted, then let cool. When the chocolate is cool but not set, dip the cookies diagonally into it to coat halfway, then place on the wire racks to set. You may find it easier to do this with tongs.

96 Lemon & white chocolate fingers

Replace the orange rind and juice with lemon rind and juice and use melted white chocolate to coat the cookies halfway.

Orange & lemon cookies

1 cup butter, softened
¾ cup superfine sugar
1 egg yolk, lightly beaten
2 cups all-purpose flour
pinch of salt
finely grated rind of 1 orange
finely grated rind of 1 lemon

FOR DECORATING
1 tbsp lightly beaten egg white
1 tbsp lemon juice
1 cup confectioners' sugar
few drops of yellow food coloring
few drops of orange food coloring
about 15 lemon gummy slices
about 15 orange gummy slices

Place the butter and sugar in a large bowl and beat together until light and fluffy, then beat in the egg yolk. Sift together the flour and salt into the mixture and stir until combined. Halve the dough and knead the orange rind into one half and the lemon rind into the other. Shape into balls, wrap, and chill for 30–60 minutes.

Preheat the oven to 375°F/190°C. Line 2 large baking sheets with parchment paper. Unwrap the orange-flavored dough and roll out between 2 sheets of parchment paper. Cut out rounds with a 2½-inch/6-cm plain cutter and place them on a baking sheet, spaced well apart. Repeat with the lemon-flavored dough and cut out crescents. Place them on the other baking sheet, spaced well apart.

Bake in the preheated oven for 10–15 minutes, or until golden brown. Let cool for 5–10 minutes, then transfer to wire racks to cool completely.

To decorate, mix the egg white and lemon juice together. Gradually beat in the confectioners' sugar until smooth. Spoon half the frosting into another bowl. Stir yellow food coloring into one bowl and orange into the other. Leave the cookies on the racks. Spread the frosting over the cookies and decorate with jelly slices. Let set.

98 Raspberry cookies

Omit the citrus rind from the dough and replace the orange and yellow food coloring with red food coloring. Top the cookies with raspberry gummy slices.

1 cup butter, softened
¾ cup superfine sugar
1 egg yolk, lightly beaten
1 oz/25 g preserved ginger, finely
   chopped, plus 2 tsp syrup from the jar

2 cups all-purpose flour
pinch of salt
3 oz/85 g dried bananas, finely chopped
15 chocolate caramels

Place the butter and sugar in a large bowl and beat together until light and fluffy, then beat in the egg yolk, ginger, and ginger syrup. Sift together the flour and salt into the mixture, add the bananas, and stir until thoroughly combined. Halve the dough, shape into balls, wrap in plastic wrap, and chill in the refrigerator for 30–60 minutes.

Preheat the oven to 375°F/190°C. Line 2 large baking sheets with parchment paper. Unwrap the dough and roll it out between 2 sheets of parchment paper. Cut out cookies with a 2½-inch/6-cm fluted round cutter and place half of them on the baking sheets, spaced well apart. Place a chocolate caramel in the center of each cookie, then top with the remaining cookies and pinch the edges of the rounds together.

Bake in the preheated oven for 10–15 minutes, or until light golden. Cool for 5–10 minutes, then transfer to wire racks to cool completely.

2 tbsp raisins
½ cup orange juice or rum
1 cup butter, softened
¾ cup superfine sugar
1 egg yolk, lightly beaten

2 cups all-purpose flour
pinch of salt
¾ cup dried bananas, finely chopped

Place the raisins in a bowl, pour in the orange juice or rum, and let soak for 30 minutes. Drain the raisins, reserving any remaining liquid.

Preheat the oven to 375°F/190°C. Line 2 large baking sheets with parchment paper. Place the butter and sugar in a large bowl and beat together until light and fluffy, then beat in the egg yolk and 2 teaspoons of the reserved orange juice. Sift together the flour and salt into the mixture, add the raisins and dried bananas, and stir until combined.

Place tablespoons of the mixture into heaps on the baking sheets, spaced well apart, then flatten them gently.

Bake in the preheated oven for 12–15 minutes, or until golden. Let cool on the baking sheets for 5–10 minutes, then transfer the cookies to wire racks to cool completely.

101 *Banana & coconut cookies*

Replace the raisins with ½ cup dry unsweetened coconut.

1 cup butter, softened
¾ cup superfine sugar
2 tsp finely grated orange rind
1 egg yolk, lightly beaten
2 tsp vanilla extract
1¾ cups all-purpose flour
¼ cup unsweetened cocoa
pinch of salt
3½ oz/100 g semisweet chocolate,
finely chopped

CHOCOLATE FILLING
½ cup heavy cream
7 oz/200 g white chocolate,
broken into pieces
1 tsp orange extract

Preheat the oven to 375°F/190°C. Line 2 large baking sheets with parchment paper.

Place the butter, sugar, and orange rind in a large bowl and beat together until light and fluffy. Beat in the egg yolk and vanilla. Sift together the flour, cocoa, and salt into the mixture, then add the chocolate and stir well. Scoop up tablespoons of the dough, roll into balls, and place on the baking sheets, spaced well apart. Gently flatten and smooth the tops with the back of a spoon.

Bake in the preheated oven for 10–15 minutes, or until light golden. Let cool on the baking sheets for 5–10 minutes, then transfer to wire racks to cool completely.

To make the filling, bring the cream to a boil in a small saucepan, then remove the pan from the heat. Stir in the chocolate until the mixture is smooth, then stir in the orange extract. When the mixture is completely cool, sandwich the cookies together in pairs.

103 *With semisweet chocolate*

For the chocolate filling, replace the white chocolate with semisweet chocolate and sift over cocoa to finish.

104 *With semisweet & white chocolate*

Replace half the white chocolate with melted semisweet chocolate to make 2 fillings. Fill half the sandwiches with white filling and sift over confectioners' sugar. Fill the remaining cookies with semisweet chocolate filling and sift over cocoa.

105 Snickerdoodles

1 cup butter, softened
¾ cup superfine sugar
2 large eggs, lightly beaten
1 tsp vanilla extract
3 cups all-purpose flour
1 tsp baking soda
½ tsp freshly grated nutmeg

pinch of salt
⅓ cup pecans, finely chopped

CINNAMON COATING
1 tbsp superfine sugar
2 tbsp ground cinnamon

Place the butter and sugar in a large bowl and beat together until light and fluffy, then beat in the eggs and vanilla extract. Sift together the flour, baking soda, nutmeg, and salt into the mixture, add the pecans, and stir until thoroughly combined. Shape the dough into a ball, wrap in plastic wrap, and chill in the refrigerator for 30–60 minutes.

Preheat the oven to 375°F/190°C. Line 2 large baking sheets with parchment paper.

For the coating, mix the sugar and cinnamon in a shallow dish. Scoop up tablespoons of the dough and roll into balls. Roll each ball in the cinnamon mixture and place on the baking sheets, spaced well apart. Bake in the preheated oven for 10–12 minutes, or until golden brown. Cool for 5–10 minutes, then transfer to wire racks to cool completely.

106 Chocodoodles

Add 2 tablespoons of cocoa to the dough and roll the cookies in 2 tablespoons of superfine sugar mixed with 1 tablespoon of cocoa before baking.

107 Melt-in-the-middles

3 oz/85 g semisweet chocolate,
    broken into pieces
8 tbsp butter, softened
¾ cup superfine sugar
1 egg yolk, lightly beaten
2 tsp vanilla extract
2 cups all-purpose flour
1 tbsp unsweetened cocoa
pinch of salt

FILLING
1 egg white
¼ cup superfine sugar
1 cup dry unsweetened coconut
1 tsp all-purpose flour
2 tbsp plumped dried papaya,
    finely chopped

Preheat the oven to 375°F/190°C. Line 2 large baking sheets with parchment paper.

To make the middle filling, whisk the egg white in a large bowl until soft peaks form, then gradually whisk in the sugar. Gently fold in the coconut, flour, and papaya and set aside.

Place the chocolate in a heatproof bowl, set the bowl over a saucepan of gently simmering water, and heat until melted, then remove from the heat. Place the butter and sugar in a large bowl and beat together until light and fluffy, then beat in the egg yolk and vanilla extract. Sift together the flour, cocoa, and salt into the mixture and stir until thoroughly combined. Stir in the melted chocolate and knead lightly.

Roll out the dough between 2 sheets of parchment paper to ¼–⅜ inch/5–8 mm thick. Cut out rounds with a 2¾-inch/7-cm fluted round cutter and place them on the baking sheets. Using a 1¼-inch/ 3-cm plain round cutter, cut out the centers and remove them. Bake for 8 minutes, then remove from the oven and lower the temperature to 325°F/160°C. Spoon the filling mixture into the center of the cookies. Place a sheet of foil over each baking sheet, crumpled so that it doesn't touch the cookies, to stop the filling mixture from browning.

Bake for an additional 15–20 minutes, or until the middles are firm. Let cool on the baking sheets for 5–10 minutes, then transfer the cookies to wire racks to cool completely.

108 Crunchy muesli cookies

8 tbsp unsalted butter, softened,
    plus extra for greasing
½ cup raw brown sugar
1 tbsp honey
heaping ¾ cup self-rising flour
pinch of salt
⅓ cup plumped dried apricots, chopped

heaping ¼ cup dried figs, chopped
1⅓ cups rolled oats
1 tsp milk (optional)
¼ cup golden raisins or cranberries
scant ½ cup walnut halves, chopped

Preheat the oven to 325°F/160°C. Grease 2 large baking sheets. Place the butter, sugar, and honey in a saucepan and heat over low heat until melted. Mix to combine. Sift together the flour and salt into a large bowl and stir in the apricots, figs, and oats. Pour in the butter and sugar mixture and mix to form a dough. If it is too stiff, add a little milk.

Divide the dough into 24 pieces and roll each piece into a ball. Place 12 balls on each baking sheet and press flat to a diameter of 2½ inches/ 6 cm. Mix the golden raisins and walnuts together and press into the cookies. Bake in the preheated oven for 15 minutes, swapping the sheets halfway through. Let cool on the baking sheets.

109 With nutty topping

Chop ⅔ cup mixed nuts and use to top the cookies before baking.

110 Really large coconut macaroons

2 large egg whites
heaping ½ cup superfine sugar
1⅔ cups dry unsweetened coconut
8 candied cherries

Preheat the oven to 350°F/180°C. Line 2–3 large baking sheets with rice paper.

Place the egg whites in a large bowl and whisk until soft peaks form and they hold their shape but are not dry. Add the sugar to the egg whites and, using a large metal spoon, fold in until incorporated. Add the coconut and fold into the mixture. Place 8 heaping tablespoons of the mixture onto the baking sheets and place a cherry on top of each macaroon.

Bake in the preheated oven for 15–20 minutes, or until lightly golden brown around the edges. Leave on the baking sheets for 2–3 minutes, then transfer the macaroons to a wire rack to cool completely.

111 Nutty macaroons

Finely chop ⅓ cup almonds, hazelnuts, macadamia nuts, pecans, or walnuts and add to the mixture with the coconut.

1 cup butter, softened
¾ cup superfine sugar
1 egg yolk, lightly beaten
2 cups all-purpose flour
pinch of salt
½ tsp apple pie spice
⅓ cup plumped dried apple,
    finely chopped

½ tsp ground ginger
⅓ cup plumped dried pears,
    finely chopped
¼ cup slivered almonds
1 egg white, lightly beaten
raw brown sugar, for sprinkling

Place the butter and sugar in a large bowl and beat together until light and fluffy, then beat in the egg yolk. Sift together the flour and salt into the mixture and stir until combined. Transfer half the dough to another bowl. Add the apple pie spice and dried apple to one bowl and mix well. Shape into a ball, wrap in plastic wrap, and chill for 30–60 minutes.

Add the ginger and dried pear to the other bowl and mix well. Shape into a ball, wrap in plastic wrap, and chill for 30–60 minutes.

Preheat the oven to 375°F/ 190°C. Line 2 large baking sheets with parchment paper.

Unwrap the apple-flavored dough and roll out between 2 sheets of parchment paper to about ⅛ inch/3 mm thick. Cut out cookies with a sun-shaped cutter and place them on the baking sheet.

Repeat with the pear-flavored dough. Cut out cookies with a star-shaped cutter and place them on the other baking sheet.

Bake in the preheated oven for 5 minutes, then remove the star-shaped cookies from the oven

and sprinkle with the slivered almonds. Bake for an additional 5–10 minutes. Remove the cookies from the oven but do not turn off the heat. Brush the apple suns with a little egg white and sprinkle with raw brown sugar, then bake for an additional 2–3 minutes. Let all the cookies cool for 5–10 minutes, then transfer them onto wire racks to cool completely.

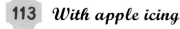

113 *With apple icing*

Replace the slivered almonds, egg white, and sugar topping with an apple-flavored basic icing made by sifting 1 cup confectioners' sugar into a bowl and beating in 1½ tablespoons of apple juice with a drop of green food coloring. Spread onto the cooled cookies.

2 tbsp butter, softened, plus extra
    for greasing
2 tbsp candied orange peel
2 tbsp superfine sugar

2 tbsp all-purpose flour
¼ cup ground almonds
finely grated rind of 1 small orange
1 tsp orange juice

Preheat the oven to 350°F/180°C. Grease several large baking sheets. Very finely chop the candied orange peel.

Place the butter and sugar in a large bowl and whisk together until pale and creamy. Add the flour, ground almonds, grated orange rind, and juice and mix well together.

Place teaspoonfuls of the mixture onto the baking sheets, spacing them well apart. Bake in the preheated oven for 7–8 minutes, or until lightly golden brown around the edges. Leave on the baking sheets for 2–3 minutes, then transfer the cookies to wire racks to cool completely.

Citrus crescents

*7 tbsp butter, softened, plus extra
   for greasing*
heaping ⅓ cup superfine sugar
1 egg, separated
*scant 1½ cups all-purpose flour, plus
   extra for dusting*

finely grated rind of 1 orange
finely grated rind of 1 lemon
finely grated rind of 1 lime
2–3 tbsp orange juice

Preheat the oven to 400°F/200°C. Lightly grease 2 large baking sheets. Place the butter and sugar in a large bowl and beat together until light and fluffy, then gradually beat in the egg yolk. Sift the flour into the creamed mixture and mix until thoroughly combined. Add the orange, lemon, and lime rinds with enough of the orange juice to form a soft dough.

Roll the dough out on a lightly floured work surface and cut out rounds with a 3-inch/7.5-cm cookie cutter. Make crescent shapes by cutting away a quarter of each round. Re-roll the trimmings to make about 25 crescents. Place the crescents on the baking sheets and prick the surface of each crescent with a fork. Lightly whisk the egg white in a small bowl and brush it over the cookies.

Bake in the preheated oven for 12–15 minutes, or until golden brown. Let the cookies cool on a wire rack before serving.

116 *With lemon cream*

Make a double quantity of the cookies. Prepare the lemon cream by beating 9 tablespoons of softened butter with 1½ cups confectioners' sugar and 1 teaspoon of finely grated lemon rind, 1 tablespoon of lemon juice, and ½ teaspoon of lemon oil, then use to sandwich the cookies together.

Chocolate temptations

5½ tbsp butter, plus extra for greasing
12½ oz/365 g semisweet chocolate
1 tsp strong coffee
2 eggs
¼ cup light brown sugar
1⅓ cups all-purpose flour
¼ tsp baking powder

pinch of salt
2 tsp almond extract
heaping ½ cup Brazil nuts, chopped
heaping ½ cup hazelnuts, chopped
1½ oz/40 g white chocolate

Preheat the oven to 350°F/180°C. Grease 2 large baking sheets. Place 8 oz/225 g of the semisweet chocolate with the butter and coffee into a heatproof bowl, set the bowl over a saucepan of simmering water, and heat until the chocolate is almost melted. Remove and stir until smooth.

Beat the eggs in a bowl until fluffy, then gradually whisk in the sugar until thick. Add the chocolate to the egg mixture and stir to combine. Sift the flour, baking powder, and salt into a separate bowl and stir into the chocolate. Chop 3 oz/85 g of the semisweet chocolate into pieces and stir into the mixture. Stir in the almond extract and nuts. Place

24 tablespoonfuls of the dough onto the baking sheets. Bake in the preheated oven for 16 minutes. Transfer the cookies to a wire rack to cool. To decorate, melt the remaining semisweet chocolate and white chocolate, in turn, then spoon into pastry bags and pipe lines on the cookies. Let set.

Rose flower cookies

1 cup butter, softened
heaping 1 cup superfine sugar
1 large egg, lightly beaten
1 tbsp rose water
2 cups all-purpose flour
1 tsp baking powder
pinch of salt

FROSTING
1 egg white
scant 2¼ cups confectioners' sugar
2 tsp all-purpose flour
2 tsp rose water
few drops of pink food coloring

Place the butter and sugar in a large bowl and beat together until light and fluffy, then beat in the egg and rose water. Sift together the flour, baking powder, and salt into the mixture and stir until combined. Shape the dough into a log, wrap in plastic wrap, and chill in the refrigerator for 1–2 hours.

Preheat the oven to 375°F/190°C. Line 2–3 baking sheets with parchment paper.

Unwrap the dough, cut into thin slices with a sharp serrated knife and place on the baking sheets, spaced well apart.

Bake in the preheated oven for 10–12 minutes, or until light golden brown. Let cool on the baking sheets for 10 minutes, then transfer the cookies to wire racks to cool completely.

To make the frosting, use a fork to lightly beat the egg white in a bowl. Sift in half the confectioners' sugar and stir well, then sift in the remaining confectioners' sugar and flour and mix in enough rose water to make a smooth, easy-to-spread frosting. Stir in a few drops of pink food coloring.

Leave the cookies on the racks. Gently spread the frosting over them and let set.

119 *Violet flower cookies*

Omit the rose water and pink food coloring. Tint the frosting with a little lavender or violet food coloring, then spread the frosting on the cookies and scatter over 3 oz/85 g chopped crystallized violets.

120 *Zebra cookies*

2 oz/55 g semisweet chocolate,
  broken into pieces
1 cup all-purpose flour
1 tsp baking powder
1 egg
¼ cup superfine sugar

¼ cup sunflower oil, plus extra
  for greasing
½ tsp vanilla extract
2 tbsp confectioners' sugar
1 small package milk chocolate disks
1 small package white chocolate disks

Place the chocolate in a heatproof bowl, set the bowl over a saucepan of gently simmering water, and heat until melted. Let cool. Sift the flour and baking powder together. Meanwhile, place the egg, sugar, oil, and vanilla extract in a large bowl and whisk together. Whisk in the cooled, melted chocolate until well blended, then gradually stir in the sifted flour. Cover the bowl and chill in the refrigerator for at least 3 hours.

Preheat the oven to 375°F/190°C. Oil 1–2 large baking sheets with the oil.

Using your hands, shape tablespoonfuls of the dough into log shapes, each measuring about 2 inches/5 cm. Roll the logs generously in the confectioners' sugar, then place on the baking sheets, spaced well apart. Bake in the preheated oven for 15 minutes, or until firm. As soon as the cookies are done, place 3 chocolate disks down the center of each, alternating the colors. Transfer to a wire rack and let cool.

121 *With zebra icing*

Sift 1 cup confectioners' sugar into a bowl, add 1 tablespoon of water, and mix until smooth. Set aside one quarter and tint with black food coloring. Use the white icing to ice the cookies then add stripes with the black icing and let set.

½ cup raisins
⅔ cup rum
1 cup butter, softened
¾ cup superfine sugar
1 egg yolk, lightly beaten
2 cups all-purpose flour
pinch of salt

ORANGE FILLING
1½ cups confectioners' sugar
6 tbsp butter, softened
2 tsp finely grated orange rind
1 tsp rum
few drops of yellow food coloring
(optional)

Place the raisins in a bowl, pour in the rum, and let soak for 15 minutes, then drain, reserving the remaining rum.

Preheat the oven to 375°F/190°C. Line 2 large baking sheets with parchment paper.

Place the butter and sugar in a large bowl and beat together until light and fluffy, then beat in the egg yolk and 2 teaspoons of the reserved rum. Sift together the flour and salt into the mixture, add the raisins, and stir until thoroughly combined.

Scoop up tablespoons of the dough and place them on the baking sheets, spaced well apart. Flatten gently and smooth the tops with the back of a spoon.

Bake in the preheated oven for 10–15 minutes, or until light golden brown. Let cool on the baking sheets for 5–10 minutes, then transfer the cookies to wire racks to cool completely.

To make the orange filling, sift the confectioners' sugar into a bowl, add the butter, orange rind, rum, and food coloring, if using, and beat well until smooth. Spread the filling over half the cookies and top with the remaining cookies.

123 *With semisweet chocolate filling*

Replace the orange filling with a chocolate filling made by heating ½ cup heavy cream to boiling point and pouring over 4½ oz/125 g chopped semisweet chocolate, then mixing until smooth. Cool and chill until thick, then use to sandwich the cookies together.

124 *Gingersnaps* MAKES 30

2½ cups self-rising flour
pinch of salt
1 cup superfine sugar
1 tbsp ground ginger
1 tsp baking soda

9 tbsp butter, plus extra
  for greasing
¼ cup dark corn syrup
1 egg, lightly beaten
1 tsp grated orange rind

Preheat the oven to 325°F/160°C. Lightly grease several large baking sheets.

Sift together the flour, salt, sugar, ginger, and baking soda into a large bowl. Heat the butter and dark corn syrup together in a saucepan over very low heat until the butter has melted. Let cool slightly, then pour it onto the dry ingredients. Add the egg and orange rind and mix thoroughly to form a dough. Using your hands, carefully shape the dough into 30 even-size balls.

Place the balls on the baking sheets, spaced well apart, then flatten them slightly with your fingers.

Bake in the preheated oven for 15–20 minutes, then carefully transfer the cookies to a wire rack to cool.

125 *Extra ginger gingersnaps*

Drain 3 balls of preserved ginger in syrup, chop finely, and add to the dough before baking.

Fennel & angelica cookies

1 cup butter, softened
¼ cup superfine sugar
1 egg yolk, lightly beaten
1 tbsp finely chopped angelica

2 cups all-purpose flour
pinch of salt
1 tbsp fennel seeds

Place the butter and sugar in a large bowl and beat together until light and fluffy, then beat in the egg yolk and angelica. Sift together the flour and salt into the mixture, add the fennel seeds, and stir until thoroughly combined. Shape the dough into a log, wrap in plastic wrap, and chill in the refrigerator for 30–60 minutes.

Preheat the oven to 375°F/190°C. Line 2 large baking sheets with parchment paper. Unwrap the dough, cut into ½-inch/1-cm slices with a sharp serrated knife, and place them on the baking sheets, spaced well apart. Bake in the preheated oven for 12–15 minutes, or until golden.

Let cool on the baking sheets for 5–10 minutes, then transfer the cookies to wire racks to cool completely.

127 *Fennel, lemon & angelica cookies*

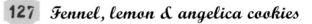

Add 1 teaspoon of finely grated lemon rind and ½ teaspoon of lemon oil to the dough.

Sticky ginger cookies

1 cup butter, softened
¾ cup superfine sugar
1 egg yolk, lightly beaten
2 oz/55 g preserved ginger, coarsely
*   chopped, plus 1 tbsp syrup from the jar*

2 cups all-purpose flour
pinch of salt
⅓ cup semisweet chocolate chips

Place the butter and sugar in a large bowl and beat together until light and fluffy, then beat in the egg yolk and ginger syrup. Sift together the flour and salt into the mixture, add the preserved ginger and chocolate chips, and stir until thoroughly combined. Shape the mixture into a log, wrap in plastic wrap, and chill in the refrigerator for 30–60 minutes.

Preheat the oven to 375°F/190°C. Line 2 large baking sheets with parchment paper.

Unwrap the log, cut it into ¼-inch/5-mm slices with a sharp serrated knife, and place them on the baking sheets, spaced well apart. Bake in the preheated oven for 12–15 minutes, or until golden brown.

Let cool on the baking sheets for 5–10 minutes, then transfer the cookies to wire racks to cool completely.

129 *Sticky citrus cookies*

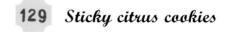

Replace the chocolate chips with chopped candied peel.

Blackstrap molasses & spice drizzles

scant 1 cup butter, softened
2 tbsp blackstrap molasses
¾ cup superfine sugar
1 egg yolk, lightly beaten
2 cups all-purpose flour
1 tsp ground cinnamon
½ tsp grated nutmeg
½ tsp ground cloves

pinch of salt
2 tbsp chopped walnuts

ICING
1 cup confectioners' sugar
1 tbsp hot water
few drops of yellow food coloring
few drops of pink food coloring

Place the butter, blackstrap molasses, and sugar in a large bowl and beat together until fluffy, then beat in the egg yolk.

Sift together the flour, cinnamon, nutmeg, cloves, and salt into the mixture, add the walnuts, and stir until thoroughly combined. Halve the dough, shape into balls, wrap in plastic wrap, and chill for 30–60 minutes.

Preheat the oven to 375°F/190°C. Line 2 baking sheets with parchment paper. Unwrap the dough and roll out between 2 sheets of parchment paper to about ¼ inch/5 mm thick. Cut out rounds with a 2½-inch/6-cm fluted cutter and place them on the baking sheets.

Bake in the preheated oven for 10–15 minutes, or until firm. Let cool on the baking sheets for 5–10 minutes, then transfer the cookies to wire racks to cool completely.

To make confectioners' sugar then gradually stir in the hot water until it has the consistency of thick cream. Spoon half the icing into another bowl and stir a few drops of yellow food coloring into one bowl and a few drops of pink food coloring into the other. Leave the cookies on the racks and, using teaspoons, drizzle the yellow icing over them in one direction and the pink icing over them at right angles. Let set.

131 *Syrup drizzles*

Replace the blackstrap molasses with dark corn syrup and decorate the cookies with the icing, leaving out the food coloring.

132 *Cinnamon & orange crisps*

MAKES ABOUT 30

1 cup butter, softened
1 cup superfine sugar
finely grated rind of 1 orange
1 egg yolk, lightly beaten

4 tsp orange juice
2 cups all-purpose flour
pinch of salt
2 tsp ground cinnamon

Place the butter, ¾ cup of the sugar, and the orange rind in a large bowl and beat together until light and fluffy, then beat in the egg yolk and 2 teaspoons of the orange juice. Sift together the flour and salt into the mixture and stir until thoroughly combined. Shape the dough into a ball, wrap in plastic wrap, and chill for 30–60 minutes.

Unwrap the dough and roll out between 2 sheets of parchment paper into a 12-inch/30-cm square. Brush with the remaining orange juice and sprinkle with cinnamon. Lightly roll with the rolling pin. Roll up the dough like a jelly roll. Wrap in plastic wrap and chill for 30 minutes.

Preheat the oven to 375°F/190°C. Line 2 large baking sheets with parchment paper.

Unwrap the dough and cut into thin slices, then place on the baking sheets, spaced well apart. Bake in the preheated oven for 10–12 minutes. Let cool for 5–10 minutes, then transfer to wire racks to cool completely.

133 *With white chocolate coating*

Place 5½ oz/150 g white chocolate in a heatproof bowl, set the bowl over a saucepan of gently simmering water, and heat until melted. Dip the cooled cookies to coat half of each one and let set on a wire rack.

Chocolate chip & cinnamon cookies

1 cup butter, softened
¼ cup superfine sugar
1 egg yolk, lightly beaten
2 tsp orange extract
2 cups all-purpose flour
pinch of salt

heaping ½ cup semisweet
  chocolate chips

CINNAMON COATING
1½ tbsp superfine sugar
1½ tbsp ground cinnamon

Preheat the oven to 190°C/375°F/Gas Mark 5. Line 2 large baking sheets with parchment paper. Place the butter and sugar in a large bowl and beat together until light and fluffy, then beat in the egg yolk and orange extract. Sift together the flour and salt into the mixture, add the chocolate chips and stir until thoroughly combined.

To make the cinnamon coating, mix the sugar and cinnamon together in a shallow dish. Scoop out tablespoons of the cookie dough, roll them into balls, then roll them in the cinnamon mixture to coat. Place them on the baking sheets, spaced well apart.

Bake in the preheated oven for 12–15 minutes, or until golden brown. Leave to cool on the baking sheets for 5–10 minutes, then transfer the cookies to wire racks to cool completely.

135 White chocolate & spice cookies

Replace the semisweet chocolate chips with heaping ½ cup white chocolate chips and replace the cinnamon with 1 tablespoon of apple pie spice and ½ teaspoon of ground nutmeg.

---

136 Papaya & cashew nut cookies

1 cup butter, softened
¼ cup superfine sugar
1 egg yolk, lightly beaten
2 tsp lime juice
2 cups all-purpose flour

pinch of salt
½ cup plumped dried papaya, chopped
⅔ cup cashew nuts, finely chopped

Place the butter and sugar in a large bowl and beat together until light and fluffy, then beat in the egg yolk and lime juice.

Sift together the flour and salt into the mixture, add the papaya, and stir until thoroughly combined.

Spread out the cashew nuts in a shallow dish. Shape the dough into a log and roll in the nuts to coat. Wrap the dough in plastic wrap, and chill in the refrigerator for 30–60 minutes.

Preheat the oven to 375°F/ 190°C. Line 2 large baking sheets with parchment paper.

Unwrap the dough, cut into slices with a sharp serrated knife and place them on the baking sheets, spaced well apart.

Bake in the preheated oven for 12–15 minutes, or until light golden. Let cool on the baking sheets for 5–10 minutes, then transfer the cookies to wire racks to cool completely.

137 With cashew frosting

Beat 6 tablespoons of butter, 1 cup confectioners' sugar, and heaping ⅓ cup cashew nut butter together until smooth and spread over the cooled cookies.

1 cup butter, softened
¾ cup superfine sugar
finely grated rind of 1 lime
1 egg yolk, lightly beaten
2 tsp white rum
2 cups all-purpose flour
pinch of salt

½ cup plumped dried peaches, chopped

ICING
1¼ cups confectioners' sugar
2 tbsp white rum

Preheat the oven to 375°F/190°C. Line 2 baking sheets with parchment paper.

Place the butter, sugar, and lime rind in a large bowl and beat together until light and fluffy, then beat in the egg yolk and rum. Sift together the flour and salt into the mixture, add the peaches, and stir until thoroughly combined. Scoop up tablespoons of the dough and place them on the baking sheets, then flatten gently. Bake in the preheated oven for 10–15 minutes, or until light golden brown. Let cool on the baking sheets for 5–10 minutes, then transfer the cookies to wire racks to cool completely.

Sift the confectioners' sugar into a bowl and stir in enough rum until the mixture is the consistency of thick cream. Leave the cookies on the wire racks and drizzle the icing over them with a teaspoon. Let set.

139 *With peach icing*

Omit the dried peaches from the cookie dough and instead stir them into a double quantity of icing. Spoon the icing onto the cooled cookies, then spread to cover and let set.

1 cup butter, softened
¾ cup superfine sugar
1 egg yolk, lightly beaten
2 tsp almond extract
2 cups all-purpose flour
pinch of salt

⅓ cup plumped dried peaches,
    finely chopped
⅓ cup plumped dried pears,
    finely chopped
4 tbsp plum jam

Preheat the oven to 375°F/190°C. Line 2 large baking sheets with parchment paper. Place the butter and sugar in a large bowl and beat together until light and fluffy, then beat in the egg yolk and almond extract. Sift together the flour and salt into the mixture, add the dried fruit, and stir until thoroughly combined.

Scoop up tablespoons of the mixture, roll them into balls, and place on the baking sheets, spaced well apart. Make a hollow in the center of each with the dampened handle of a wooden spoon and fill the hollows with the jam. Bake in the preheated oven for 12–15 minutes, or until light golden brown.

Leave to cool on the baking sheets for 5–10 minutes, then transfer the cookies to wire racks to cool completely.

141 *Extra peachy cookies*

Replace the plum jam with peach preserve and serve topped with chopped fresh peach.

heaping ⅔ cup unsalted butter, softened
½ cup confectioners' sugar
½ tsp vanilla extract

heaping 1 cup all-purpose flour
pinch of salt
⅓ cup candied cherries, chopped

Preheat the oven to 375°F/190°C. Place the butter and sugar in a large bowl and beat together until light and fluffy. Add the vanilla extract and beat until combined. Sift in the flour and salt in batches, mixing well between each addition. Add the cherries and mix well.

Spoon the mixture into a pastry bag fitted with a 1-inch/2.5-cm star tip and pipe rings onto 2 large nonstick baking sheets. Bake in the preheated oven for 8–10 minutes, or until light golden. Let cool on a wire rack.

143 *With cherry frosting*

Make a butter frosting with 6 tablespoons of butter beaten with 1⅓ cups confectioners' sugar and adding ¼ cup chopped candied cherries. Pipe the frosting onto the cookies and decorate with pieces of angelica.

1 cup butter, softened
¼ cup superfine sugar
1 egg yolk, lightly beaten
2 tsp almond extract

1⅓ cups all-purpose flour
pinch of salt
heaping ½ cup ground almonds
⅓ cup pistachios, finely chopped

Place the butter and sugar in a large bowl and beat together until light and fluffy, then beat in the egg yolk and almond extract. Sift together the flour and salt into the mixture, add the ground almonds, and stir until thoroughly combined. Halve the dough, shape into balls, wrap in plastic wrap, and chill in the refrigerator for 30–60 minutes.

Preheat the oven to 375°F/190°C. Line 2 large baking sheets with parchment paper. Unwrap the dough and roll out between 2 sheets of parchment paper to about ⅛ inch/3 mm thick. Sprinkle half the pistachios over each piece of dough and roll lightly with the rolling pin. Cut out cookies with a heart-shaped cutter and place them on the baking sheets, spaced well apart.

Bake in the preheated oven for 10–12 minutes. Let cool for 5–10 minutes, then transfer the cookies to wire racks to cool completely.

145 *With pistachio cream*

Whisk scant 1 cup heavy cream to soft peaks with 2 tablespoons of confectioners' sugar and ½ teaspoon of green food coloring. Fold in ½ cup chopped pistachios and spoon into a bowl, then use as a dip for the cookies.

8 tbsp butter, softened
scant ⅔ cup superfine sugar
scant ⅔ cup light brown sugar
2 large eggs, lightly beaten
1 tsp vanilla extract
2 cups all-purpose flour
1 tsp baking soda
10½ oz/300 g chocolate chunks

Preheat the oven to 350°F/180°C. Line several large baking sheets with parchment paper.

Place the butter and sugars in a large bowl and whisk together until pale and creamy. Whisk the eggs and vanilla extract into the mixture until smooth. Sift in the flour and baking soda and beat together until well mixed. Stir in the chocolate chunks.

Drop 12 large spoonfuls of the batter onto the baking sheets, spacing them well apart.

Bake in the preheated oven for 15–20 minutes, or until set and golden brown. Let cool on the baking sheets for 2–3 minutes, then transfer the cookies to a wire rack and let cool completely.

147 *Giant chocolate chip cookies*

Replace the chocolate chunks with chocolate chips. These can be semisweet, milk, or white chocolate, or use some of each.

148 *Indulgent chocolate chunk cookies*

Scatter 3½ oz/100 g chocolate chunks over the top of the cookies before baking in the oven.

1 cup butter, softened
¾ cup superfine sugar, plus extra
    for coating
1 tbsp (3–4 tea bags) camomile or
    camomile and lime flower infusion tea
1 egg yolk, lightly beaten

1 tsp vanilla extract
2 cups all-purpose flour
pinch of salt

Place the butter and sugar in a large bowl and beat together until light
and fluffy. If using tea bags, remove the tea leaves from the bags. Stir the
tea into the butter mixture, then beat in the egg yolk and vanilla extract.
Sift together the flour and salt into the mixture and stir until thoroughly
combined. Shape the dough into a log. Spread out the extra sugar in a
shallow dish and roll the log in the sugar to coat. Wrap in plastic wrap
and chill in the refrigerator for 30–60 minutes.

Preheat the oven to 375°F/190°C. Line 2 large baking sheets with
parchment paper.

Unwrap the log, cut into ¼-inch/5-mm slices with a sharp serrated
knife and place them on the baking sheets, spaced well apart. Bake in
the preheated oven for 10 minutes, or until golden. Let cool on the
baking sheets for 5–10 minutes, then transfer the cookies to wire racks
to cool completely.

150 *Lemon verbena cookies*

*Replace the camomile tea with lemon verbena tea and add ½ teaspoon
of finely grated lemon rind to the dough.*

⅔ cup unsalted butter, softened
¾ cup superfine sugar
1⅓ cups self-rising flour

1–2 tbsp milk
½ tsp vanilla extract
2 cups pecans

Preheat the oven to 375°F/190°C. Line 2 large baking sheets with
parchment paper. Place the butter and sugar in a large bowl and beat
together until light and fluffy. Sift in the flour and beat to combine. Add
1 tablespoon of milk and the vanilla extract and mix to form a dough,
adding more milk if the dough is too stiff.

Set aside 20 pecan halves. Chop the remaining pecans and knead in
to the dough. Divide the dough into 20 and roll each piece into a ball.
Place 10 balls on each baking sheet, spaced well apart. Press down to a
thickness of ½ inch/1 cm, then press a pecan half into the center of each
cookie. Bake in the preheated oven for 10–15 minutes. Let the cookies
cool on the baking sheets.

Cappuccino cookies

2 envelopes instant cappuccino
1 tbsp hot water
1 cup butter, softened
¾ cup superfine sugar
1 egg yolk, lightly beaten
2 cups all-purpose flour

pinch of salt

TOPPING
6 oz/175 g white chocolate,
    broken into pieces
unsweetened cocoa, for dusting

Empty the cappuccino envelopes into a small bowl and stir in the hot, but not boiling, water to make a paste. Place the butter and sugar in a large bowl and beat together until light and fluffy, then beat in the egg yolk and cappuccino paste. Sift together the flour and salt into the mixture and stir until combined. Halve the dough, shape into balls, wrap in plastic wrap, and chill for 30–60 minutes.

Preheat the oven to 375°F/190°C. Line 2 large baking sheets with parchment paper. Unwrap the dough and roll it out between 2 sheets of parchment paper. Cut out cookies with a 2½-inch/6-cm round cutter and place them on the baking sheets, spaced well apart. Bake in the preheated oven for 10–12 minutes, or until golden brown. Let cool for 5–10 minutes, then transfer to wire racks to cool completely.

Place the wire racks over a sheet of parchment paper. Place the chocolate into a heatproof bowl, set the bowl over a saucepan of gently simmering water, and heat until melted. Let cool, then spoon the chocolate over the cookies. Let set, then dust lightly with cocoa.

153 With coffee bean topping

Replace the cocoa with 3½ oz/100 g crushed chocolate-covered coffee beans, scatter them over the melted white chocolate topping, and let set.

154 Cinnamon & caramel cookies

MAKES ABOUT 25

1 cup butter, softened
¾ cup superfine sugar
1 egg yolk, lightly beaten
1 tsp vanilla extract
2 cups all-purpose flour

1 tsp ground cinnamon
½ tsp allspice
pinch of salt
25–30 caramels

Preheat the oven to 375°F/190°C. Line 2 large baking sheets with parchment paper. Place the butter and sugar in a large bowl and beat together until light and fluffy, then beat in the egg yolk and vanilla extract. Sift together the flour, cinnamon, allspice, and salt into the mixture and stir until thoroughly combined.

Scoop up tablespoons of the dough, shape into balls, and place on the baking sheets, spaced well apart. Bake in the preheated oven for 8 minutes. Place a caramel on top of each cookie and bake for an additional 6–7 minutes. Let cool on the baking sheets for 5–10 minutes, then transfer to wire racks to cool completely.

155 Lemon & candy cookies

Replace the cinnamon and allspice with 1 teaspoon of finely grated lemon rind. Replace the caramels with 25 lemon-flavored hard candies.

Almond crunchies

1 cup butter, softened
¾ cup superfine sugar
1 egg yolk, lightly beaten
½ tsp almond extract

1⅔ cups all-purpose flour
pinch of salt
1½ cups blanched almonds, chopped

Place the butter and sugar in a large bowl and beat together until light and fluffy, then beat in the egg yolk and almond extract. Sift together the flour and salt into the mixture, add the almonds, and stir until thoroughly combined. Halve the dough, shape it into balls, wrap in plastic wrap, and chill in the refrigerator for 30–60 minutes.

Preheat the oven to 375°F/190°C. Line 2–3 baking sheets with parchment paper.

Shape the dough into about 50 small balls, flatten them slightly between the palms of your hands, and place them on the baking sheets, spaced well apart. Bake in the preheated oven for 15–20 minutes, or until golden brown. Let cool on the baking sheets for 5–10 minutes, then transfer to wire racks to cool completely.

157 With marzipan filling

Cut 3½ oz/100 g marzipan into small cubes and press one piece into the middle of each cookie. Form the dough around the marzipan to completely enclose and bake as before.

---

158 Almond & raspberry jam drops

1 cup butter, softened
¾ cup superfine sugar
1 egg yolk, lightly beaten
2 tsp almond extract
2 cups all-purpose flour

pinch of salt
heaping ⅓ cup almonds, toasted
 and chopped
½ cup chopped candied peel
4 tbsp raspberry jam

Preheat the oven to 375°F/190°C. Line 2 baking sheets with parchment paper. Place the butter and sugar in a large bowl and beat together until light and fluffy, then beat in the egg yolk and almond extract. Sift together the flour and salt into the mixture, add the almonds and candied peel, and stir until thoroughly combined.

Scoop out tablespoons of the dough and shape into balls with your hands, then place them on the baking sheets, spaced well apart. Use the dampened handle of a wooden spoon to make a hollow in the center of each cookie and fill with raspberry jam. Bake in the preheated oven for 12–15 minutes, or until golden brown. Let cool for 5–10 minutes, then transfer to wire racks to cool completely.

159 Almond & strawberry jam drops

Replace the candied peel with ⅓ cup chopped dried strawberries and replace the raspberry jam with strawberry jam.

Nutty drizzles

heaping ¾ cup butter, plus extra
    for greasing
scant 1½ cups raw brown sugar
1 egg
1 cup all-purpose flour
1 tsp baking powder
1 tsp baking soda
1½ cups rolled oats

1 tbsp bran
1 tbsp wheat germ
¾ cup mixed nuts, toasted and
    coarsely chopped
scant 1¼ cups semisweet chocolate chips
¾ cup mixed raisins and golden raisins
6 oz/175 g semisweet chocolate,
    coarsely chopped

Preheat the oven to 350°F/180°C. Grease 2 large ba[...] butter, sugar, and egg in a large bowl and beat together until lig[...] fluffy. Sift in the flour, baking powder, and baking soda. Add the oats, bran, and wheat germ and mix together until well combined. Stir in the nuts, chocolate chips, and raisins. Place 24 rounded tablespoons of the dough on the baking sheets.

Bake in the preheated oven for 12 minutes, or until golden brown. Let cool on wire racks.

Meanwhile, place the chocolate pieces in a heatproof bowl, set the bowl over a saucepan of gently simmering water, and heat until melted. Stir the chocolate, then let cool slightly. Use a spoon to drizzle the chocolate in waves over the cookies, or spoon it into a pastry bag and pipe zigzag lines over the cookies.

161 *With nut chocolate topping*

Add ¼ cup chopped mixed nuts to the melted chocolate and spread over the cookies.

162 *Cashew & poppy seed cookies*

MAKES ABOUT 20

1 cup butter, softened
¼ cup superfine sugar
1 egg yolk, lightly beaten
2 cups all-purpose flour

1 tsp ground cinnamon
pinch of salt
¼ cup cashew nuts, chopped
2–3 tbsp poppy seeds

Place the butter and sugar in a large bowl and beat together until light and fluffy, then beat in the egg yolk. Sift together the flour, cinnamon, and salt into the mixture, add the nuts, and stir until combined. Shape the dough into a log. Spread out the poppy seeds in a dish and roll the log in them until coated. Wrap in plastic wrap and chill in the refrigerator for 30–60 minutes.

Preheat the oven to 375°F/190°C. Line 2 large baking sheets with parchment paper.

Unwrap the dough, cut into ½-inch/1-cm slices with a sharp serrated knife, and place them on the baking sheets. Bake in the preheated oven for 12 minutes, or until golden brown. Let cool on the baking sheets for 5–10 minutes, then transfer to wire racks to cool completely.

163 *Cashew nut cookies*

Omit the poppy seeds and roll the dough in 1½ cups finely chopped cashew nuts.

scant ¾ cup butter, plus extra for greasing
1 cup light brown sugar
1 egg
½ cup all-purpose flour, plus extra
    for dusting (optional)
1 tsp baking soda
pinch of salt
½ cup whole wheat flour
1 tbsp bran
heaping 1¼ cups semisweet
    chocolate chips
scant 2¼ cups rolled oats
1 tbsp strong coffee
⅔ cup hazelnuts, toasted
    and coarsely chopped

Preheat the oven to 375°F/190°C. Grease 2 large baking sheets. Place the butter and sugar in a large bowl and beat together until light and fluffy. Add the egg and beat well. Sift together the all-purpose flour, baking soda, and salt into another bowl, then add in the whole wheat flour and bran. Mix in the egg mixture, then stir in the chocolate chips, oats, coffee, and hazelnuts and mix well.

Place 24 rounded tablespoons of the dough on the baking sheets, spaced well apart. Alternatively, with lightly floured hands, break off pieces of the dough and roll into 24 balls, place on the baking sheets, and flatten.

Bake in the preheated oven for 16–18 minutes, or until golden brown. Let cool for 5 minutes, then transfer to a wire rack to cool completely.

165 *With ice cream filling*

Remove a tub of semisweet chocolate ice cream from the freezer and let soften at room temperature. Tip into a bowl and add 2 tablespoons of Kahlúa coffee liqueur and beat together. Use to sandwich the baked cookies together, then freeze the cookies for 10 minutes until firm. Makes 12.

1 cup rolled oats
¾ cup all-purpose flour
½ tsp baking soda
pinch of salt
4½ tbsp unsalted butter, softened
½ cup light brown sugar
¼ cup granulated sugar
1 large egg
½ tsp vanilla extract
1 cup raisins

Preheat the oven to 375°F/190°C. Place the oats in a food processor and pulse briefly, then tip into a bowl and sift in the flour, baking soda, and salt and stir together.

Place the butter and sugars in a large bowl and beat together until light and fluffy. Place the egg and vanilla extract in a separate bowl and whisk together, then add to the butter and mix well. Add the flour mixture, mix together, then add the raisins and mix thoroughly.

Divide the dough into 15 balls and place on 2 large nonstick baking sheets, spaced well apart. Press the cookies into rough rounds. Bake in the preheated oven for 12 minutes, or until golden brown. Let cool for 5 minutes, then transfer to a wire rack to cool completely.

167 *Jumbo oat, apricot & prune chippers*

Replace the raisins with heaping ½ cup chopped dried apricots and heaping ½ cup chopped pitted prunes.

168 Mocha walnut cookies

8 tbsp butter, softened, plus extra
   for greasing
heaping ½ cup dark brown sugar
scant ½ cup superfine sugar
1 tsp vanilla extract
1 tbsp instant coffee granules, dissolved
   in 1 tbsp hot water

1 egg
1¼ cups all-purpose flour
½ tsp baking powder
¼ tsp baking soda
⅓ cup milk chocolate chips
½ cup walnut halves, coarsely chopped

Preheat the oven to 350°F/180°C. Grease 2 large baking sheets. Place the butter and sugars in a large bowl and beat together until light and fluffy. Place the vanilla, coffee, and egg in a separate bowl and whisk together. Gradually add the coffee mixture to the butter and sugar, beating until fluffy. Sift the flour, baking powder, and baking soda into the mixture and fold in carefully. Fold in the chocolate chips and walnuts.

Spoon heaping teaspoons of the dough onto the baking sheets, spaced well apart. Bake in the preheated oven for 10–15 minutes, or until crisp on the outside but soft inside. Let cool on the baking sheets for 2 minutes, then transfer to wire racks to cool completely.

169 With mocha frosting

Sift 1 cup confectioners' sugar into a bowl. Stir ½ teaspoon of instant espresso powder, ½ teaspoon of cocoa, and 1 tablespoon of boiling water together until smooth. Add to the confectioners' sugar and mix to a smooth frosting, spread over the cookies, and let set on a wire rack.

170 Almond tuilles

1 tsp peanut oil, for greasing
6 tbsp unsalted butter, softened
heaping ⅓ cup superfine sugar

heaping ⅓ cup all-purpose flour
pinch of salt
¾ cup slivered almonds

Preheat the oven to 400°F/200°C and oil 2 large baking sheets with the oil. Place the butter and sugar in a large bowl and beat together until light and fluffy. Sift together the flour and salt and fold into the mixture, then add the almonds and mix together.

Drop 12 teaspoons of batter on each baking sheet, spaced well apart, and spread into flat ovals with the back of a spoon.

Bake in the preheated oven for 5 minutes, or until golden. While the cookies are still warm, lift each one in turn and drape over a wooden rolling pin to make a curved shape. Leave for 1 minute to harden, then transfer to a wire rack to cool completely.

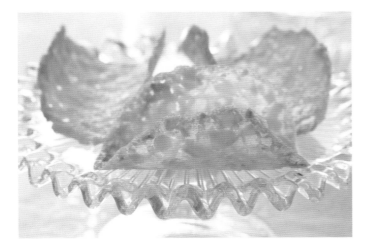

171 With chocolate coating

Place 5½ oz/150 g semisweet chocolate in a heatproof bowl, set the bowl over a saucepan of gently simmering water, and heat until melted. Dip each tuille into the melted chocolate and let set on parchment paper.

lovers' cookie brittle

...greasing
...unsalted butter, softened
1 cup granulated sugar
1 tsp vanilla extract
2 cups all-purpose flour

pinch of salt
1 cup milk chocolate chips
1 cup pecans, chopped
1 cup almonds, toasted
    and chopped

Preheat the oven to 375°F/190°C. Grease a 15 x 10-inch/38 x 25-cm/ jelly roll pan with the oil. Place the butter and sugar in a large bowl and beat together until light and fluffy, then stir in the vanilla extract. Sift together the flour and salt into the mixture and beat until combined. Mix in ½ cup of the chocolate chips and the nuts and press the dough into the pan, making sure the dough fills the pan and is evenly spread. Bake in the preheated oven for 20–25 minutes, or until golden. Let cool in the pan.

Place the remaining chocolate chips in a heatproof bowl, set the bowl over a saucepan of gently simmering water, and heat until melted. Drizzle the chocolate over the cookie brittle and let set, then break the brittle into irregular pieces.

173 Lemon almond brittle

Omit the chocolate and nuts, and add the finely grated rind of 2 lemons to the dough before pressing into the pan. Top with 1½ cups slivered almonds and bake as before. Cool and break into pieces.

174 Dark & white chocolate cookies

heaping ¾ cup butter, softened, plus
    extra for greasing
1 cup superfine sugar
½ tsp vanilla extract
1 large egg

1⅔ cups all-purpose flour
pinch of salt
1 tsp baking soda
⅔ cup white chocolate chips
4 oz/115 g semisweet chocolate chips

Preheat the oven to 350°F/180°C. Grease 2 large baking sheets. Place the butter, sugar, and vanilla extract in a large bowl and beat together. Gradually beat in the egg until the mixture is light and fluffy. Sift the flour, salt, and baking soda over the mixture and fold in. Fold in the chocolate chips.

Drop heaping teaspoonfuls of the batter onto the baking sheets, spaced well apart. Bake in the preheated oven for 10–12 minutes, or until crisp outside but still soft inside.

Let cool on the baking sheets for 2 minutes, then transfer the cookies to wire racks to cool completely.

175 Dark chocolate & hazelnut cookies

Replace the white chocolate chips with chopped toasted hazelnuts.

1 cup butter, softened
¼ cup superfine sugar
1 egg yolk, lightly beaten
2 tbsp finely chopped preserved ginger,
    plus 2 tsp syrup from the jar
heaping 1¾ cups all-purpose flour
¼ cup unsweetened cocoa
½ tsp ground cinnamon
pinch of salt
scant 2 cups vanilla, chocolate,
    or coffee ice cream

Place the butter and sugar in a large bowl and beat together until light and fluffy, then beat in the egg yolk, ginger, and ginger syrup. Sift together the flour, cocoa, cinnamon, and salt into the mixture and stir until combined. Halve the dough, shape into balls, wrap in plastic wrap, and chill for 30–60 minutes.

Preheat the oven to 375°F/ 190°C. Line 2 large baking sheets with parchment paper. Unwrap the dough and roll out between 2 sheets of parchment paper. Cut out cookies with a 2½-inch/6-cm fluted round cutter and place them on the baking sheets, spaced well apart.

Bake in the preheated oven for 10–15 minutes, or until light golden brown. Let cool for 5–10 minutes, then transfer to wire racks to cool completely.

Remove the ice cream from the freezer about 15 minutes before serving, to allow it to soften. Put a generous scoop of ice cream on half the cookies and top with the remaining cookies. Press together gently so that the filling spreads to the edges. If not serving immediately, wrap the cookies individually in foil and store in the freezer.

177 *Chocolate mint sandwiches*

Replace the preserved ginger in the cookie dough with 1 teaspoon of peppermint extract, then fill the cookies with chocolate chip ice cream.

1 cup butter, softened
¼ cup superfine sugar
1 egg yolk, lightly beaten
2 tsp vanilla extract
1⅔ cups all-purpose flour
pinch of salt
½ cup ground walnuts
½ cup walnuts, finely chopped
confectioners' sugar, for
    dusting (optional)

COFFEE CREAM
6 tbsp butter, softened
1¼ cups confectioners' sugar
1½ tsp strong black coffee

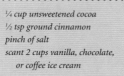

Place the butter and sugar in a large bowl and beat together until light and fluffy, then beat in the egg yolk and vanilla extract. Sift together the flour and salt into the mixture, add the ground walnuts, and stir until combined. Halve the dough, shape into balls, wrap in plastic wrap, and chill in the refrigerator for 30–60 minutes.

Preheat the oven to 375°F/ 190°C. Line 2 baking sheets with parchment paper. Unwrap the dough and roll out between 2 sheets of parchment paper. Cut out cookies with a 2½-inch/6-cm fluted round cutter and place them on the baking sheets, spaced well apart.

Bake in the preheated oven for 10–15 minutes, or until light golden brown. Let cool on the baking sheets for 5–10 minutes, then transfer the cookies to wire racks to cool completely.

To make the coffee cream, place the butter and confectioners' sugar in a bowl and beat together until smooth and thoroughly combined, then beat in the coffee.

Sandwich the cookies together in pairs with the coffee cream, then press together gently so that the cream oozes out of the sides. Smooth the sides with a dampened finger. Spread out the chopped walnuts in a shallow dish and roll the cookies in them to coat the sides of the coffee cream filling. Dust the tops with sifted confectioners' sugar, if liked.

179 *Chocolate cream & walnut cookies*

Replace the coffee with 1 teaspoon of cocoa.

The gooiest chocolate cookies

8 tbsp unsalted butter, softened
1¼ cups light brown sugar
1 large egg, lightly beaten
2 tsp vanilla extract
2 cups all-purpose flour

1 tbsp unsweetened cocoa
1 tsp baking soda
1 tsp salt
7 oz/200 g semisweet chocolate, chopped
5½ oz/150 g milk chocolate, chopped

Preheat the oven to 350°F/180°C. Line 2 large baking sheets with nonstick parchment paper. Place the butter and sugar in a large bowl and beat together until light and fluffy. Place the egg and vanilla extract in a separate bowl and whisk together, then gradually add to the butter mixture and beat until smooth. Mix in the flour, cocoa, baking soda, and salt until well combined. Add 3½ oz/100 g each of the semisweet and milk chocolates, then mix well.

Spoon 6 heaping tablespoons of the batter onto each baking sheet, spacing them well apart. Divide the remaining chocolate among the cookies and press in lightly.

Bake in the preheated oven for 15–17 minutes. Let cool on the baking sheets for 5 minutes, then transfer to a wire rack to cool.

181 With extra chocolate

Place 5½ oz/150 g milk chocolate in a heatproof bowl, set the bowl over a saucepan of gently simmering water, and heat until melted. Let cool for a few minutes, then spread over the cold cookies and let set.

Peanut butter cookies

8 tbsp butter, softened, plus extra
   for greasing
½ cup crunchy peanut butter
heaping ½ cup superfine sugar
heaping ½ cup dark brown sugar
1 egg, lightly beaten

½ tsp vanilla extract
½ cup all-purpose flour
½ tsp baking soda
½ tsp baking powder
pinch of salt
1⅓ cups rolled oats

Preheat the oven to 350°F/180°C. Grease 3 large baking sheets. Place the butter and peanut butter in a bowl and beat together, then beat in the sugars. Gradually beat in the egg and vanilla extract. Sift the flour, baking soda, baking powder, and salt into the mixture, add the oats, and stir until just combined.

Place spoonfuls of the dough on the baking sheets, spaced well apart, and flatten slightly with a fork. Bake in the preheated oven for 12 minutes, or until lightly browned. Let cool on the baking sheets for 2 minutes, then transfer to wire racks to cool completely.

183 With banana filling

Spread a cookie with smooth peanut butter and top with thin slices of banana tossed in lemon juice, then top with a second cookie and sandwich together. Makes about 13.

184 Carrot cake cookies

8 tbsp butter, softened
scant ⅓ cup superfine sugar
heaping ⅓ cup light brown sugar
1 large egg
½ tsp vanilla extract
heaping 1 cup all-purpose flour

½ tsp baking soda
½ tsp ground cinnamon
½ cup finely grated carrot
¼ cup walnut halves, chopped
heaping ¼ cup dry unsweetened coconut

Preheat the oven to 375°F/190°C. Line several large baking sheets with parchment paper.

Place the butter and sugars in a large bowl and whisk together until pale and creamy. Whisk the egg and vanilla extract into the mixture until smooth. Sift in the flour, baking soda, and cinnamon, then beat together until well mixed. Add the grated carrot, chopped walnuts, and coconut to the mixture and mix well together.

Drop heaping teaspoonfuls of the batter onto the baking sheets, spaced well apart. Bake in the preheated oven for 8–10 minutes, or until lightly golden brown around the edges.

Let cool on the baking sheets for 2–3 minutes, then transfer to a wire rack to cool completely.

185 Frosted carrot cake cookies

When the cookies are cold, top with a cream cheese frosting. Put scant ¼ cup soft cream cheese, 2 tablespoons of butter, and ½ teaspoon of vanilla extract in a large bowl and beat together until smooth. Sift in 1¾ cups confectioners' sugar and beat together until combined, then spread on top of the cookies.

186 Banana & chocolate cookies

MAKES ABOUT 20

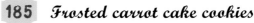

9 tbsp butter
⅔ cup superfine sugar
1 large egg, lightly beaten
1 ripe banana, mashed
1¼ cups self-rising flour

1 tsp apple pie spice
2 tbsp milk
3½ oz/100 g chocolate, cut into chunks
⅓ cup raisins

Preheat the oven to 375°F/190°C. Line 2 large baking sheets with parchment paper. Place the butter and sugar in a large bowl and beat together until light and fluffy. Gradually add the egg, beating well after each addition. Mash the banana and add it to the mixture, beating well until smooth.

Sift together the flour and apple pie spice into the mixture and fold in with a spatula. Add the milk to give a soft consistency, then fold in the chocolate and raisins. Drop tablespoons of the batter onto the baking sheets, spaced well apart. Bake in the center of the preheated oven for 15–20 minutes, or until lightly golden. Let cool slightly, then transfer to a wire rack to cool completely.

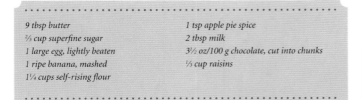

Pistachio biscotti

1 cup butter, softened
¾ cup superfine sugar
finely grated rind of 1 lemon
1 egg yolk, lightly beaten
2 tsp brandy

2 cups all-purpose flour
½ cup pistachios
pinch of salt
confectioners' sugar, for dusting

Place the butter, sugar, and lemon rind in a large bowl and beat together until light and fluffy, then beat in the egg yolk and brandy. Sift together the flour, pistachios, and salt into the mixture and stir until thoroughly combined. Shape the mixture into a log, flatten slightly, wrap in plastic wrap, and chill in the refrigerator for 30–60 minutes.

Preheat the oven to 375°F/190°C. Line 2 large baking sheets with parchment paper. Unwrap the log, cut it slightly on the diagonal into ¼-inch/5-mm slices with a sharp serrated knife, and place them on the baking sheets.

Bake in the oven for 10 minutes, or until golden brown. Let cool for 5–10 minutes, then transfer to wire racks to cool completely. Dust with sifted confectioners' sugar.

188 Hazelnut biscotti

Replace the pistachios with hazelnuts and replace the lemon rind with the finely grated rind of 1 orange.

189 Zesty lemon biscotti

butter, for greasing
2 cups all-purpose flour, plus extra
    for dusting
1 tsp baking powder

¾ cup superfine sugar
½ cup blanched almonds
2 large eggs, lightly beaten
finely grated rind and juice of 1 lemon

Preheat the oven to 350°F/180°C. Grease a large baking sheet. Sift the flour and baking powder into a large bowl. Add the sugar, almonds, beaten eggs, lemon rind, and juice to the flour and mix together to form a soft dough. Turn the dough onto a lightly floured work surface and, with floured hands, knead for 2–3 minutes, or until smooth.

Divide the dough in half and shape each portion into a log shape measuring about 1½ inches/4 cm in diameter. Place the logs on the baking sheet and flatten until each is about 1 inch/2.5 cm thick.

Bake in the preheated oven for 25 minutes, or until lightly golden brown. Remove from the oven. Reduce the oven temperature to 300°F/150°C. Let cool for 15 minutes.

Using a serrated knife, cut the baked dough into ½-inch/1-cm thick slices and place cut-side down on ungreased baking sheets. Bake for an additional 10 minutes. Turn and bake for 10–15 minutes, or until golden brown and crisp. Transfer to a wire rack and let cool and harden.

190 Zesty orange & walnut biscotti

Replace the grated lemon rind and juice with orange rind and juice. Replace the almonds with chopped walnut halves.

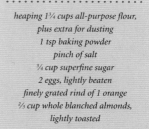

heaping 1¾ cups all-purpose flour,
plus extra for dusting
1 tsp baking powder
pinch of salt
¾ cup superfine sugar
2 eggs, lightly beaten
finely grated rind of 1 orange
⅔ cup whole blanched almonds,
lightly toasted

Preheat the oven to 350°F/180°C. Lightly dust a large baking sheet with flour. Sift the flour, baking powder, and salt into a bowl. Add the sugar, eggs, and orange rind and mix to form a dough. Knead in the almonds.

Roll the dough into a ball, cut in half, roll out each portion into a log about 1½ inches/4 cm in diameter, and place the logs on the baking sheet. Bake in the preheated oven for 10 minutes. Let cool for 5 minutes.

Using a serrated knife, cut the baked dough into ½-inch/1-cm thick diagonal slices. Arrange the slices on ungreased baking sheets and return to the oven for 15 minutes, or until slightly golden. Transfer to a wire rack to cool and harden.

192 *Vanilla & almond biscotti*

Omit the grated orange rind and add 2 teaspoons of vanilla extract to the mixture with the eggs. Sprinkle 2 tablespoons of chopped blanched almonds on top of the logs before baking and press lightly into the dough.

193 *Rose water biscotti*

Omit the orange rind and add 2 teaspoons of rose water to the mixture with the eggs. Before baking, mix 1 egg white with 1 teaspoon of water. Brush over the dough and sprinkle 1 tablespoon of superfine sugar over each log.

194 *Spicy nut biscotti*

3½ tbsp butter, softened, plus extra
  for greasing
¼ cup superfine sugar
¼ cup light brown sugar
2 large eggs, lightly beaten
2 cups all-purpose flour, plus extra
  for dusting

1¼ tsp baking powder
¼ tsp ground cinnamon
¼ tsp grated nutmeg
¼ tsp ground ginger
⅔ cup blanched almonds, chopped

Preheat the oven to 375°F/190°C. Grease a large baking sheet. Place the butter and sugars in a large bowl and whisk together until pale and creamy. Whisk the eggs into the mixture. Sift in the flour, baking powder, cinnamon, nutmeg, and ginger. Add the chopped almonds, reserving 2 tablespoons, and mix together to form a soft dough.

Turn the dough onto a lightly floured work surface and, with floured hands, knead for 2–3 minutes, or until smooth. Divide the dough in half and shape each portion into a log shape measuring about 1½ inches/ 4 cm in diameter.

Place the logs on the baking sheet and flatten until each is about 1 inch/2.5 cm thick.

Sprinkle the reserved almonds on top of the logs and press into the dough.

Bake in the preheated oven for 20–25 minutes, or until lightly golden brown. Remove from the oven and let cool for 15 minutes. Reduce the oven temperature to 325°F/160°C. Using a serrated knife, cut the baked dough into ½-inch/1-cm thick slices and place, cut-side down, on ungreased baking sheets. Bake for an additional 10 minutes. Turn and bake for another 10–15 minutes, or until lightly golden brown and crisp. Transfer to a wire rack to cool and harden.

195 *Cherry & almond biscotti*

3½ tbsp butter, softened, plus extra
  for greasing
½ cup superfine sugar
1 large egg, lightly beaten
scant 1½ cups all-purpose flour,
  plus extra for dusting
1¼ tsp baking powder
3½ oz/100 g candied cherries, halved
¼ cup blanched almonds,
  coarsely chopped

Preheat the oven to 375°F/190°C. Grease a large baking sheet. Place the butter and sugar in a large bowl and whisk together until pale and creamy. Whisk in the egg. Sift the flour and baking powder into the mixture. Add the cherries and chopped almonds and mix together to form a soft dough. Turn the dough onto a lightly floured work surface and, with floured hands, knead for 2–3

minutes, or until smooth. Divide the dough in half and shape each portion into a log shape measuring about 1½ inches/4 cm in diameter. Place the logs on the baking sheet and flatten until each is about 1 inch/2.5 cm thick.

Bake in the preheated oven for 20–25 minutes, or until lightly golden brown. Remove from the oven and let cool for 15 minutes. Reduce the oven temperature to

325°F/160°C. Using a serrated knife, cut the baked dough into ½-inch/1-cm thick slices and place, cut-side down, on ungreased baking sheets. Bake for an additional 10 minutes. Turn and bake for another 10–15 minutes until crisp. Transfer to a wire rack to cool and harden.

196 *Mixed berry biscotti*

Replace the cherries with ½ cup dried cranberries and ¼ cup dried blueberries.

Traditional oatcakes

2⅔ cups rolled oats, plus extra
for dusting
½ tsp baking soda

½ tsp salt
1 tbsp unsalted butter, melted
⅔ cup warm water

Preheat the oven to 350°F/180°C. Place the oats and baking soda into a large bowl and stir in the salt, making a well in the middle. Pour the melted butter and warm water into the oatmeal mixture and mix together to form a soft dough.

Roll the dough out on a work surface lightly dusted with oats. Cut out oatcakes with a cookie cutter. Re-roll any trimmings and cut out more oatcakes. Place the oatcakes on 2 large nonstick baking sheets.

Bake in the preheated oven for 20 minutes, turning them 3 times while cooking. Leave on a wire rack to cool completely.

198 ## Cranberry oatcakes

Add ¼ cup chopped dried cranberries to the dough and knead in before rolling out the dough.

199

Gingerbread people

8 tbsp butter, plus extra for greasing
3¼ cups all-purpose flour, plus
extra for dusting
2 tsp ground ginger
1 tsp pumpkin pie spice
2 tsp baking soda
heaping ¼ cup dark corn syrup
heaping ½ cup dark brown sugar
1 egg, lightly beaten

FOR DECORATING
raisins
candied cherries
¼ cup confectioners' sugar
3–4 tsp water

Preheat the oven to 325°F/160°C. Grease 3 large baking sheets. Sift the flour, ginger, pumpkin pie spice, and baking soda into a large bowl. Place the butter, dark corn syrup, and dark brown sugar in a saucepan over low heat and stir until melted. Pour onto the dry ingredients and add the egg. Mix together to form a dough. The dough will be sticky to start with, but will become firmer as it cools.

Roll out the dough on a lightly floured work surface to about ⅛ inch/3 mm thick and cut out gingerbread people shapes. Place the shapes on the baking sheets. Reknead and reroll the trimmings and cut out more shapes. Decorate with raisins for the eyes and pieces of candied cherry for the mouths.

Bake in the preheated oven for 15–20 minutes, or until firm and lightly browned. Let cool on the baking sheets for a few minutes, then transfer the cookies to wire racks to cool completely.

Place the confectioners' sugar and water in a small bowl and mix together until it is thick. Place the icing in a small pastry bag fitted with a plain tip and use to pipe buttons and bows onto the cookies.

200 ## Gingerbread ark

Use animal cookie cutters to make gingerbread animals. Make a Noah's Ark gift box with 2 gingerbread people and several animals.

Index